An Incomplete Guide
to Basic Research Methods
and Data Collection
for Counsellors

Pete Sanders
and
Damian Liptrot

PCCS BOOKS
Manchester

First Published in 1993
PCCS BOOKS
3 Chelford Rd
Old Trafford
Manchester
M16 0BJ

An Incomplete Guide to Basic Research Methods
and Data Collection for Counsellors

ISBN   1 898059 02 0

Cover Design by Peter Kneebone
Printed by Printoff Graphic Arts Ltd. Alexander House,
Lomeshaye Road, Nelson, Lancashire

Contents

Contents

Introduction, Acknowledgements and Warnings

Introduction

We have tried to rise to the challenge of writing a book for readers who have no background in data collection and research and may also feel a little shaky about the prospect of solving equations. At the same time we wanted to provide a refresher for those who took a social science course some time in the distant past and have forgotten nearly everything about methodology. We also wanted to write a book that was academically credible whilst being accessible. Could we tread the line between making the issues comprehensible without resorting to baby talk? Only you the reader will be able to answer that and before you can you will have to read the book. It is worth noting that both of us had trouble with maths at school and statistics wasn't our favourite subject as undergraduate psychologists, yet we both went on to be teachers and examiners in the subject.

The book is intended to be read in a number of different ways depending upon your experience. We have gone to some trouble to put the ideas in what we think is a logical order. There's a storyline, or plot, if you like. If you are a research 'novice' and you try dipping in to the book, you may miss some of the development of the ideas and may have to backtrack to find the beginning of some of the examples that tend to weave their way around the chapters. If the book has a mission it is to say "Don't be afraid of the numbers, they're just a smoke screen. Research is about common-sense and logic, and counselling research needs a healthy dose of both plus a large measure of energy and enthusiasm."

As we proceeded, we kept extending the boundaries of the book but realised that we would have to stop somewhere. We finally decided to go as far as collecting, summarising and describing data. Making inferences from your data is left to the companion volume 'An Incomplete Guide to Inferential Statistics for Counsellors'. The two books should provide most counselling investigators with a good enough kit to get started on the research trail and keep their noses clean.

Scattered around the book are Help! boxes which we like to think of as reassuring notes to say that there's a bit coming up which the novice might find difficult and which can sometimes be missed out if you want. They're not intended to be Panic! boxes which create problems by drawing your attention to possible difficulties; the idea is that they're more like Don't Panic! boxes anticipating areas of concern and acknowledging that the lay person may find what follows a bit confusing. The trick is to stick with it as long as possible, or failing any light dawning at the end of the tunnel, skip it until you feel up to it at a later date.

Acknowledgements

We urge you to read the warnings that follow very carefully, but before you do, we would like to gratefully acknowledge the following: Firstly The Association for the Teaching of Psychology for permission to use material from their pamphlet 'Ethics in Psychological Research' by Graham Davies, Geoff Haworth and Sue Hirschler. Secondly we are indebted to Dave Jordan for wrestling with our diagrams and charts until we had finally stopped changing our minds. Damian would like to thank his mum Eileen (as proof reader and guinea pig) and his wife Eileen (as muse and thesaurus). Pete would like to thank Hannah, Jake, Sam and particularly Rosie and Maggie, for putting up with him during his confinement.

Warnings

1. This book contains numbers and as such, may be offensive to counsellors!

2. We have a language problem. We use 'I', 'we' and 'you' throughout the book in a not entirely consistent way. This is because Pete wrote some chapters, Damian wrote others and both of us wanted to keep an approachable style which involved you, the reader. So, generally 'I' means the author of the chapter, 'we' means you (the reader) and us (the authors) together, and 'you' means you the reader(s). We think it makes sense as you read it.

3. All of the examples are fictional. None of the research projects used or the numbers given are either real or related to research in progress or completed. In order to make the examples more relevant we have referred to the British Association for Counselling, counsellors in general, clients, psychiatrists, women, men and other groups. All references to research and results concerning any such group are invented.

4. You may end up enjoying research and data collection.

Pete Sanders and Damian Liptrot
Manchester 1993

1 Asking Questions

Throughout this book we are trying to relate the business of research to everyday examples that crop up in most peoples' lives, putting the subject in everyday language, eliminating or explaining technical terms and jargon. The same is true for the chapter headings as we hope will become obvious. We could have called Chapter 3 'Descriptive Statistics', but that may have put readers off. By the same token, we could have started the book with a chapter called 'Generating Hypotheses', but again that doesn't relate very closely to peoples' lives and besides, what is a hypothesis anyway?

As each of us goes around the world we try to understand the workings of our world and so we ask questions. "Who are you?" "How much is that?" "Where did that come from?" "What is the meaning of this?" "How does this work?" "Why did that happen?" And to quote the popular song by the Talking Heads "How did I get here?" Clearly these questions vary in difficulty, and research describes the process by which we try to answer some of these questions.

When considering the best way of getting to an answer, we find that in research as in life itself, there is considerable disagreement over which way is best. I can hear even now the exasperated cries of my maths teacher, Mr Tyson "You'll never find out the answer to the question by doing *that* Sanders."

It may seem that in some areas of life, both the question and the method of seeking an answer are strikingly obvious, but we would do well to challenge our ideas of the obvious because so much of what seems 'obvious' to us is based on cultural views which, to say the least, are local (not everyone in the world shares our culture) and temporary (how many 'civilisations' throughout history have come to grief through the complacent view that they had the 'right' answer). It has been 'obvious' to the greatest thinkers of their age that the world is flat, that it is the centre of the universe around which the stars rotate, that black people are sub-human, that children need smacking, that standards in education are falling, that counselling works, etc.

There have been many attempts to categorise the 'ways of finding things out' in the world. Although philosophers have been thinking about them for thousands of years, I'll attempt the arrogant illusion of briefly summarising the situation as it is today. There are two broad methods by which human beings come to understand the world about them, **analysis** and **synthesis.**

Analysis

Taking things or ideas apart, or separating things into their constituent parts to see how the parts fit and work together. In scientific terms this is called **reductionism**.

E.g. Trying to understand the workings of the human body by dissecting it into its constituent organs and systems and understanding their individual functions. This is the main method adopted by western science.

Synthesis

Putting things together in familiar or novel ways to see what patterns are made and to understand how they might fit and work together. This is called **holism**.

E.g. Trying to understand the workings of the human body by looking at it as a coherent, indivisible unit connected to the universe and natural forces in the world through invisible energy channels. More of an eastern tradition, it has gained in popularity in the west in recent years.

Since both of these words have common uses in our culture you would be forgiven for believing that analysis alone describes the one true process by which we come to understand the world around us. It certainly is *one* valid method to gain knowledge and I have many examples in my own experience of gaining understanding through analysis. (I learned how my bicycle worked by taking it apart and re-assembling it, seeing how the parts fitted and moved together.)

Some people argue that our technological culture perpetuates the myth that analysis is the only way, yet computer technology and theoretical physics (surely the heartland of analytical science) have recently come together through a new explanation of the universe, life and everything called *chaos theory* that is the very essence of synthesis. In this theory, order in the universe is achieved through chaos - the random combinations and interactions of very small events. When computers are instructed to mimic such chaos, the result is complex irregular patterns called *fractals* that can look like and, so it is argued, explain the origin of coastlines, snowflakes, coral reefs, leaves on trees, the pattern of small blood vessels in our lungs and so on.

We have known for some time, however, that reductionism falls down under some circumstances. When I studied psychology at university it was assumed by most psychologists that reductionism was the one true way to understand the workings of the human mind. The argument went something like this:

In order to understand, say 'psychotic mental illness', we should:
* first look at the individual mentally ill people,
* then look at their individual psychotic behaviours,
* then look at the components of that behaviour,
* then look at the biological bases of that behaviour
  (hormones, nervous system and genetics),
* then look at the chemical bases of the biological systems
  and finally,

* when we can reduce the problem no further we can eliminate psychosis by:
  i) correcting chemical imbalances (drugs),
  ii) repairing a faulty nervous system (brain surgery) and, when we develop the right technology,
  iii) adjusting genetic imperfections (screening for and terminating deviant foetuses or changing human characteristics through genetic engineering).

Now if all that sounds a bit far-fetched, the first two 'solutions' have been tried for many years with results which vary from the cautiously promising to the failing disastrously and we're not far off trying the third 'solution'. (We can already test the unborn child for many 'conditions' from Downs Syndrome to Cystic Fibrosis.) How long will it be before we can choose between not only boy or girl, but intelligent or super-intelligent, neurotic or extrovert, 'psychotic' or 'normal', gay or straight?

A 'cure' for 'psychosis' still eludes us and we are turning to synthesis in the form of holism to help our understanding of psychotic' behaviour. Not so long ago, psychologists and psychiatrists were keen on the idea of 'dualism', i.e. that mind and body were split, i.e. two separate entities. Much of the current medical model of mental illness makes this assumption at its heart. Now the same doctors are busy trying to put the body and mind back together again into one integrated whole as evidence emerges to show us that people, as Carl Rogers wrote in 1951, "...react as an organised whole..." 'Client Centred Therapy', p 487.

A psychologist trying to argue against using the results of brain surgery as a method of understanding brain function, wrote that we would not try to understand the workings of a television and its constituent parts by taking a working television, arbitrarily removing a component and observing the results. If we removed a component, then switched the television on only to see multi-coloured wavy lines on the screen and hear a loud buzzing noise, we might simplistically and erroneously conclude that the purpose of the component we had removed was to prevent coloured wavy lines and buzzing sounds. For years main the method of understanding brain function was this very technique of removing a small part of a brain and observing the results. To this day, our understanding of most of the anatomy of the human brain is based on these conclusions. (It must be said, though, that on a very crude level, the majority of the early observations are holding up quite well to modern day scrutiny using less invasive methods.)

If we are to avoid making grand mistakes in our thinking, we need to have a broad view of the 'possible' in research. Both analysis and synthesis can be valid methods of research. Although *we* can seek answers to our questions through reductionism and holism, this book is going to concentrate on one set of methods based on the gathering of **quantitative** data, i.e. *measuring things with numbers*. This in itself is a somewhat contentious issue because measuring things is associated with a particular philosophical view of the world namely,

Positivism - based on the idea that there is a fixed observable world which we all experience in a similar way. Knowledge is limited to observed facts and that which can be deduced from those observed facts. Positivism is associated with **quantitative** methods.

This view is not held by everyone. In particular it is challenged by the ideas of

Phenomenology - that our knowledge should be based on our experience, on attending to phenomena as they are directly and subjectively experienced. This viewpoint is most often associated with **qualitative** methods.

However, some researchers have recently pointed out that the use of measurement and numbers does not preclude the use of individual experience. So-called **New Paradigm Research** and **Action Research** use both qualitative, narrative methods (accounts of peoples' experiences) *and* quantitative methods. The emphasis of these new approaches is to keep the process of human experience at the centre of the enquiry whilst at the same time understanding the effects of any measuring methods on that central experience.

These new methodologies offer the following criticisms of traditional approaches:

1.Social Science research that follows a traditional method tends to be rationalistic, i.e. it *assumes* that human experiences, thoughts and feelings follow, and are the result of rational, logical, decision making processes. This turns out to be a dangerous assumption to make and the results of applying a rational methodology to irrational experience or behaviour are either:

> i) that the results do not offer useful or actionable explanations of human behaviour or
> ii) that the method imposes rationality upon the irrational human processes and thus *masks* their true nature. (This has serious implications for any view of human experience or behaviour based on rational decision making.)

2. Whenever you measure something the scale itself imposes a meaning upon the measurement. A researcher then, will only ever find what s/he is seeking because the measurements used limit and define the frame of reference of the subjects (people being studied).

3. Since the researcher has selected and defined the variables to be measured, (as well as the measurement methods in 2 above) the results will do nothing more than reproduce the researcher's frame of reference.

The conclusions of these criticisms then, are that traditional methods:
• basically mask the true nature of human experience,

• find what the researcher expects to find and
• yield explanations that will not work as predictors of human behaviour in the real world.

Does this sound familiar? Theories about how people change have, in general, failed over the years to offer practical explanations for human behaviour in everyday situations. Most recently, social scientists working in the area of health education have been disappointed to discover that traditional theories of attitude formation and change fail to predict or explain people's attitudes and behaviour surrounding safe sex, condom use and the risk of contracting HIV. The New Paradigm research now under way suggests that traditional methods asked the wrong questions in the wrong way and came up with an over simplistic, rational view of why people *know* one thing, *believe* another thing and *do* yet another. The good news for us all is that we (i.e. human beings) are much more complicated than some theorists would have us believe.

Whilst the emergence of these new methods is vitally important, the quantitative approaches are still the most frequently used in contemporary research and the skills associated with data collection and presentation are very useful in a wide range of activities from planning and evaluating systems to writing annual reports. This book is about quantitative methods and is based on the notion that whatever method is chosen, it will be worthless without accurate, valid data. We will cover this in the chapters that follow. In particular we are going to concentrate on the

Hypothetico-deductive method - a scientific method whereby we formulate a hypothesis that predicts what is going to happen in a given situation. We then set about testing the hypothesis to see if its prediction is true.

I have used the general example of *asking questions* about the world up to now, however, in research a problem is never 'asked' as a question, but stated as a hypothesis. A hypothesis is simply a statement of belief about some aspect of the world that is, as yet, unknown. It involves making a prediction that something will happen, if tested.

In life we ask questions, e.g. "What is the moon made of?"

In research we state hypotheses, e.g. "The moon is made of green cheese."

This hypothesis is a statement about something and involves the implicit prediction that if we visit the moon, we will find that it is made of green cheese. There are several reasons why we state hypotheses in research, and although there are advantages and disadvantages, the big advantage is that they simplify the issue to a manageable size.

1. On a simple level a hypothesis narrows down the possibilities which we have to investigate - when we try to answer the question there are literally millions of possibilities, whereas all we can do with an hypothesis is prove it or disprove it.

2. It is possible to verify the likelihood of our prediction being responsible for our results using statistical procedures. We can only do this if we state the problem in the form of a hypothesis. It won't work if we ask a question. (More of this in Chapter 6 called 'Research Methods'.)

3. The problem with hypotheses is that unless we hit upon the right one, we have to generate hypothesis after hypothesis,

i.e. when we send a cheese taster to the moon to test our first hypothesis, she returns to say that the moon is definitely not cheese, it tastes a bit like caviar but she's not sure. Our second hypothesis might then be that the moon is made of caviar. So up goes the fish roe expert who returns to tell us that it's not like any fish roe he's ever tasted and we generate yet another hypothesis.

Finding out what the moon really is made of could take a long time if we follow this method, and we find that in the realm of counselling research, direct observation of events is almost impossible. In the social sciences in general we have evolved methods to overcome the indirect nature of the observations we can make. To continue with the example of the moon hypothesis, it's rather like not having the technology to send a human to the moon, but being able to send a mouse and watching it through a telescope. So to find out if the moon is made of green cheese we find a mouse that we know likes green cheese and send it to the moon. We watch it through our telescope to see if it is tempted to take a nibble. To our delight we see the mouse clearly eating the moon's surface. We take photographs and publish our results to the astonishment of the scientific community and give much acclaimed lectures on the subject until some maverick scientist suggests that we hadn't checked that our mouse would only eat green cheese and nothing else. Our rival has a hypothesis that the moon is made not of green cheese at all but marzipan. And so the research continues.

In this brief example lie all the problems and challenges of quantitative research in the social sciences. These will unfold as you read the book. The remaining chapters of this book will take you through understanding measurement, presenting numbers for clarity and ease of understanding, choosing the right method to test your hypothesis and finally writing up or reporting your results in an appropriate format. We hope you find the contents and style stimulating, informative and fun.

Good' Questions and 'Bad' Questions.
All research and data collection have a social and political context. The dominant culture and government in power determine what gets funded and what doesn't. This means that at any one time there are 'Good' questions and 'Bad' questions. As counsellors we have a duty to collect data in ways that:
• do not contravene our Code of Ethics as counsellors,
  • are within the limits of principled ethical research as determined by fellow researchers, (more of this in Chapter 5 on 'Ethical

Considerations') and
• adds to human understanding in a developing, empowering way rather than a limiting, disenfranchising way.

Over the years much of social science research has failed to meet up to similar criteria. Instead of asking the general question:

"How can we construct the world so that each of us can reach our full potential?"

Social scientists have succumbed to cultural or political pressure and asked questions like:

Why are we different?"
Who is the best?"
How can we separate the best from the worst?"

If you are white, middle class, educated, able-bodied, heterosexual and male, you will have been well served by social science research questions of the latter type. The hidden part of this type of question is usually *"In order to protect the interests of the best."* For *best* read white, middle class, etc. Before collecting data, think hard why you're doing it and what the question *really* is that you're trying to answer. In any event, be sure to read Chapter 5 on Ethical Considerations' before proceeding with your investigation.

The Great Car Driving and Cooking Cover-Up
The first time I tried to learn about statistics and research methods, I failed miserably. I just couldn't understand what it was all about. It seemed incredibly complicated and anyway, I had convinced myself that I was no good at maths. Does this sound familiar?

Now I really do understand statistics and research methods, but I have never forgotten that panicky, hollow feeling of complete blankness when staring at pages of incomprehensible jargon especially when the author was explaining it in what s/he thought were 'simple terms'. I felt even worse when I realised that the explanation could not get any more simple! What should you do if you find that you simply cannot take some of this book in? Don't worry, help is at hand.

My real problem was that I *had* to pass the statistics part of my psychology degree and I needed to be able to apply statistical tests to the practical work I had been doing. What was I to do? I took comfort from what I call 'The Great Car Driving and Cooking Cover-up'. I discovered that not only could I apply the statistical tests more-or-less correctly without having the foggiest idea what they were all about, but *no-one else knew* that I couldn't tell one tail of a distribution from the other. This way of working was known and used by thousands upon thousands of social science graduates, who like me understood little, yet appeared to understand it all. So what is this Great Cover-Up?

The vast majority of car drivers do not know how cars work. Yet they are excellent drivers and get the vehicle safely from A to B without any problem whatsoever. Ask the average driver why the car goes faster when they press their foot on the accelerator and they will simply not know. They may say something about more petrol getting to the engine, but that's about it. This was roughly my state of knowledge about research methods and statistics.

I learned how to select appropriate methods by getting hold of the equivalent of a good cookbook and simply following the recipes. I didn't know why I needed baking powder in my sponge cakes, but I knew that if I followed the recipe no-one would know and they would say "What a brilliant cook!" (This level of non-understanding is fine as long as nothing goes wrong. If the car breaks down I phone the service station, if my soufflé falls flat I phone my mum.)

It is quite possible to adopt the same approach to research methods and data collection if it all seems double-dutch. Although statistical tests are beyond the scope of this book, you may find that you need to use one, so you will be relieved to learn that there are several 'cookbook' style texts listing statistical procedures and when to use them. (For further information see Appendix V.) If this book itself proves too difficult, try to adopt a 'cookbook' approach and a 'recipe following' mentality. You may wish to come back to the book after a while in the hope that it makes more sense second time round. Although we have written this book like a story - there's a logic to the order (a plot if you like), please remember that you don't have to read the chapters in order. You may like to skip to the chapter on Writing Reports and follow it recipe-style. Whichever way you choose, we would really like you to have fun!

Test yourself on Chapter 1 with these questions:

1. What is the difference between analysis and synthesis?

2. Define positivism and phenomenology.

3. What is the hypothetico-deductive method?

Discussion Point:

What sort of questions would you want to have answered about counselling? How would you ask them? How would *your* questions benefit (or not, as the case may be) from the advantages and disadvantages of positivism and phenomenology?

2 Measuring Things

Most commonplace day-to-day activities depend upon quantification - the assignment of numbers to objects or events to describe their properties. Attempting to express your requirements without numbers would be a slow, cumbersome and rather vague process.

Suppose you are driving to your counselling rooms when you notice that you need to fill your car with petrol. You put ten gallons in the tank and pay the cashier. As you put the change in your pocket you glance at your watch and realise that if you wish to speak to your colleagues before you see your first client, you'd better hurry up. How many times have you used numbers in this example? Imagine, if you can, doing all of those things without reference to numbers. Difficult if not impossible!

In fact, not only would you have used numbers, you also would have performed many of the functions and used many of the skills referred to in this book:

• measuring things,

• describing things using numbers,

• making predictions using numbers.

We are so used to describing the natural world in terms of numbers that it may come as a bit of a shock to some readers to discover that the natural world sometimes doesn't fit into a number system quite as easily as we would like. The degree to which the natural world and numbers *actually do* fit together determines the types of calculation we can do with those numbers.

For example, most of us would like to think that adding 100 to 100 gives us 200. However in certain domains of the natural world this is not true - one such domain is temperature. If we take a pan of boiling water (100°C) and add it to another pan of boiling water (100°C) the result is not a pan of water at 200°C, but a pan of water still at 100°C. Temperature doesn't add up like, say, money for example. There are special rules to govern the way numbers relate to temperature. Of course, we all know this. All of us that have ever boiled an egg or made a cup of tea, that is. We have learned the common-sense rules of numbering things in the natural world.

Scales of Measurement

So as I mentioned above, the degree to which things don't add up helps define the type of calculations we can do - clearly adding temperatures together doesn't work in the same way as, for example, adding up the money in your pocket. In the late 1940's a statistician called Stevens came up with four ways in which we can match numbers to events in the world. He called these four ways **scales of measurement** and we need to understand them before we can start measuring things in the world.

However, some of these scales may not seem to have much to do with measurement if you think that measuring something is always going to be like measuring the weight of a parcel with scales or the length of a desk with a tape measure. Remember that you are automatically making assumptions about what measuring is and how it works because you have learned the common-sense rules about measuring things. One of the really fun things about research and data collection in the social sciences is that our assumptions about what is common-sense get challenged almost every day. So suspend your assumptions and enter into the world of numbers with fresh eyes. Most of the things counsellors are interested in measuring are to do with people - what people do, think and feel. This is the most difficult, frustrating, interesting and fun area of numbers that I've ever come across. However there is some information that can help us avoid making some very simple mistakes.

1. Nominal Scale of Measurement

Definition
This is when we use numbers to name objects and events in the world. Instead of using a word to identify an object or event we use a number. The number itself has no meaning, it just tells you that the item is different from other items. Some examples are:

Everyday Examples
• Catalogue shopping - the Tefal 'County' Safety Fryer has the number 421/2894 in the current Argos Catalogue. The item before it in the catalogue (the Moulinex Masterfry Fryer) has the number 421/1541 and the item after it (the Tefal Super Safety Elite Fryer) has the number 421/2375. The numbers aren't even consecutive. They tell you nothing except that the items are different and most important of all, they allow the Argos computer to identify the product you are ordering.

• National Insurance Numbers - more everyday nominal measurement. I may be a free man but I'm also a number. It's the 'name' by which I'm known to the Department of Social Security computer. It doesn't mean anything other than 'Pete Sanders'.

• Motor Vehicle Licence Numbers - the registration number of your car is a 'name' that contains several pieces of information, including the year and region in which it was first registered.

Research Examples
• In a recent piece of research the numbers of clients choosing each of four counsellors were compared. The four counsellors were simply identified by a single number 1,2,3 and 4.

• Dividing clients up according to their gender - male and female is nominal scaling.

• Let's say we want to categorise the types of problem that clients present during their first interview. We might name the categories sexual', 'abuse', 'bereavement', etc. and number the categories 1,2,3 and so on:

Category 1 : Sexual Problems

Category 2 : Abuse

Category 3 : Bereavement

What does it enable us to do?
The nominal scale describes categorising or classifying things as the most basic form of measurement. There is no arithmetical basis for putting such categorised items into any sensible order, so all that we can do is count how many there are. The Argos computer can count how many 421/2894's were sold today, yesterday, last week, etc. We can count how many clients came to us with sexual problems, bereavement problems, etc. What we can't do is to add them up in any sensible way (421/2894 + 421/1541 or category 1 + category 3) or multiply them together to get a meaningful answer, because we're using the numbers as names.

In recent years the advent of computers has meant that we are generally more familiar with nominal scaling since computers don't understand names for categories half so well as they understand numbers. It's also easier to obtain long lists of numbers than it is to compile long lists of names.

2. Ordinal Scale of Measurement

Definition
This is when we not only use numbers to identify objects or events we also put them in an order. (*Ord*inal - *Ord*er). The number now has some meaning - the second number comes after the first and before the third. It is sometimes known as putting things in rank order or ranking and is a true measurement method. Some

examples are:

Everyday Examples
• Places in a competition - first, second and third placed songs in the Eurovision Song Contest can be placed in order, or *ranked.*

• Hotels and Restaurants - are graded in certain Guides by the number of stars or crowns they are allocated, five stars for the best down to one or no stars for the worst.

•Arranging a class of school children in order of height is ordinal scaling. (Ranking the children by height.) Of course we can go from the tallest to the shortest or the shortest to the tallest, it doesn't matter it's still ordinal scaling.

Research Examples
• We might want to know how highly our clients value our service and ask them to rank 'counsellor', 'doctor', 'solicitor', 'social worker', 'estate agent', in order of importance to them.

• A counselling service might rank their counsellors in order of popularity. (How would you do this?)

What does it enable us to do?
Ranking is the most basic way of comparing things. Before we can put things in order we have to compare them in some way - height, price, effectiveness, value, etc. Some of these qualities are subjective (the two research examples above for instance) and you will find that ordinal scaling is quite a handy and very popular way of trying to measure people's thoughts and feelings. Like nominal scaling it's difficult to do arithmetic on ranks since there's no way of knowing what the gap is between the ranks. For example, how much better is the song that came first in the Eurovision Song Contest than the song that came second? Similarly if you see a list of children's names in order of height, you can't tell from that list whether the tallest was one foot or one inch taller that the second tallest and so on down the list.

It's interesting to note that most people try to collect the most information they can in any given situation - particularly where ranks are concerned. If someone learns that Nigel Mansell won the British Grand Prix, or that Aston Villa beat Manchester United, they often want to know the margin of victory. Who won is only half the story, we also want to know by how much. It's as though we *know* the shortcomings of ranking alone.

3. Interval Scale of Measurement

Definition
Now we not only rank the items we give them numbers that indicate the gaps or *intervals* between the ranks. On an interval scale the units of measurement are equal. Interval scaling is getting to look more like our common-sense methods of numbering, but it still has a trick or two up its sleeve.

Everyday Examples
• Testing in schools, e.g. GCSE Mathematics - a score on a test of ability is an example of interval scaling. We know the gap between each unit is equal - the difference between 50 and 55 is the same as the difference between 90 and 95.

• Temperature in degrees fahrenheit or centigrade - our old friend temperature is back, still not adding up but definitely on an interval scale when measured in fahrenheit or centigrade.

Research Examples
• There are many psychometric tests around which purport to measure various human attributes. Some readers may be familiar with some which measure anxiety for example. When you obtain a score on such a test, say from 0 to 100, the intervals between each score are supposed to be equal.

• Rating Scales - these are sometimes used in counselling research to rate the performance of the counsellor from bad (non-therapeutic) to good (very therapeutic). They use various ranges; some are five-point scales, some are nine-point scales with the mid-point being 'minimally therapeutic', e.g:

1	2	3	4	5
poor		minimally therapeutic		excellent

It is generally assumed that such scales are examples of interval scaling (see below).

What does it enable us to do?
We can do some simple arithmetic on this level of scaling - addition, subtraction, multiplication, division, arithmetic mean (taking an average), square roots, etc. Interval scales can be rather seductive though and it's not what we can do with them but what we can't do with them that we need to understand. There are two problems:

1. Some scaling that looks like interval scaling isn't really. A good example of this is IQ. Many people think that Intelligence is an interval scale, but we can't really say that the gaps between the units are equal. (We could also have a good debate about whether the rating scale above is really interval scaling - what do you think?) Can we say that the difference between IQ's of 120 and 125 is the same as the difference between 50 and 55. Are 5 IQ points always the same wherever they are? However, an increase of 5 degrees Centigrade is the same wherever it is on the Centigrade scale.

2. It's OK to do the basic arithmetic on an interval scale as long as you don't want to get a ratio between two measures on it. A ratio just doesn't work on an interval scale because the scale doesn't have a **meaningful zero point**. If you score 0 on a geography test it doesn't mean that you have no geographical knowledge. Also, if you record a temperature of 0 degrees Centigrade, it doesn't mean

that there is no temperature. This is supported by the fact that when you've reached 0 on the Centigrade scale you're only at 32 on the Fahrenheit scale. So what about ratios? Well, you can't say that I know twice as much about Geography as you if I got 60 in a test and you got only 30. Nor is it true to say that it's twice as hot at 30 degrees Centigrade as at 15 degrees Centigrade. Even your body should tell you that.

4. Ratio Scale of Measurement

Definition
Now we not only have a rank with equal intervals, but also a meaningful or absolute zero - one where zero means zero quantity of the thing being measured. So a ratio scale is interval scaling with an absolute zero point.

Everyday Examples
• There are so many, length, weight, time, etc. All have equal intervals and a meaningful zero. We can 'measure' no length, no weight and no time - and these measurements indicate zero quantities of these things.

• Temperature - again! Yes, it's here too, as a ratio scale when measured in degrees Kelvin. The Kelvin scale has an absolute zero at which there is no temperature and *everything* freezes. It's a theoretical temperature that has never been achieved in practice (-273 degrees Centigrade if you're interested). This example illustrates another important point. That is that the absolute zero on a ratio scale doesn't have to be practically achievable - just theoretically possible.

Research Examples
• Let's say we want to work out the average number of sessions each client has had. We could compare self-referred clients and clients referred by another agency:

Self-referred clients average	8.4 sessions
Other agency-referred clients average	4.2 sessions

We can now say that the self-referred clients have on average twice as many counselling sessions as the other agency-referred clients. Only with ratio scaling can we do this.

• We could compare two types of helping activity with ratio scaling by looking at the average length of sessions conducted by psychiatrists and the average length of sessions conducted by counsellors:

	Psychiatrists	Counsellors
Average session length (minutes)	18.1	54.3

This time we can say that on average, counsellors' sessions last three times as long as sessions with psychiatrists.

What does it enable us to do?
That question has already been answered in the two examples above. All arithmetical calculations can be performed on a ratio scale and that allows us to apply the most powerful statistical analyses to our measurements. (More of this later.) We can do all the basic arithmetic that we could do on an interval scale and now make meaningful ratio comparisons between measurements and averages. Most people want to be able to make these powerful statements about their measurements but you must make sure you have ratio data first. Many people will want to know what will happen if they don't get it right.

1. What if I want to compare measurements in a ratio but my measurements aren't on a ratio scale?
    The short answer is - you shouldn't do it. In the real world of research, journal articles are read by folks just waiting for the author to make a mistake in his or her assumptions about the measurements. The result of getting this wrong is that your

conclusions will be erroneous and useless. In extreme cases the maths you try will just look silly - you can't take the average of male and female. However, mistakes aren't always that obvious and there are several genuinely grey areas where people argue about the nature of measurements.

2. *What if I don't know if my measurements are ordinal or interval?* This happens more often than you might think - and not only to beginners! A good example of this is the argument over whether IQ or the rating scales mentioned above are interval or ordinal scaling. In the end I may well say that I am *assuming* that the rating scale I am using is interval, even though I can't prove it, just so I can use a more powerful piece of arithmetic on it. This won't stop other researchers arguing with me and in the end even though we bring all sorts of evidence and argument to bear, we will probably still disagree. Then you, the reader will have to decide for yourself. Does my assumption make my arithmetic, and thus my conclusions, silly or not? This is where it gets to be fun!

IQ also suffers from not having a meaningful zero point, thus not being ratio scaling. If I score zero on an IQ test it doesn't mean that I have zero intelligence. Also, ratios don't work with IQ either: we wouldn't say that a person with an IQ of 150 is twice as intelligent as a person with an IQ of 75 or the same as three people with an IQ of 50 each! (Will a woman with an IQ of 150 solve the problem quicker than three women with IQ's of 50?)

On the subject of IQ it will not surprise you to learn that the publishers of Intelligence Tests claim that they are interval data and the opponents of IQ testing claim that they aren't and thus the conclusions frequently drawn by users of such tests are invalid. What do you think?

Continuous and Discrete Measurements

In addition to working out how well our measurements match a number system, we need to work out how to collect them. This is where the notion of continuous and discrete measurements comes in. It's quite simple really, either we are forced to measure in whole units (discrete) or we can use fractions or partial units (continuous).

Definition
Continuous - can be broken down into partial or fractional units. Continuous measurements can be seen as points on a line, the accuracy of the measurements doesn't depend on the size of the units.

Discrete - can only be expressed in whole units or categories. The accuracy of the measure is dependent upon the size of the unit since we have to stick within the categories available or round up or down to the nearest whole unit. The activity here is counting.

Everyday examples
• Continuous - feet & inches, pounds & ounces, minutes & seconds. These things can be **measured.**

• Discrete - categories, e.g. male & female, or putting people into age bands 0-9 yrs, 10-19 yrs, 20-29 yrs, etc. Here we are counting the number of people in each category.

Research examples
• Continuous - measuring the time each telephone counselling session takes.

• Discrete - counting the number of clients in each of four age bands:

	under 20	21-40	41-60	60+
number of clients in 1992	10	29	14	6

What does this enable us to do?
This is just another way of understanding the properties of the numbers we are collecting. Try to get used to figuring out what you can and can't do with the numbers you collect and what limits your measurements impose upon the calculations and conclusions you can draw. Most people treat all measurements as continuous. Take the famous "average" family size of 2.4 children. It's clearly impossible to have 0.4 of a child, so we must be careful and clear when expressing ideas in numbers otherwise we may find that our readers get the wrong idea.

When using discrete measurements, the kind of data we end up with is called **frequency data**, or the number of times a certain thing happens. So in the example above, we are counting the number of times or the frequency with which people aged 60+ were clients at our counselling service in 1992.

Validity and Reliability

Our measurements need another two qualities before they are worth the paper they're written on - **reliability and validity**. We'll look at these qualities one at a time:

Validity
Definition
A measure is said to be valid when it measures what it claims or intends to measure.

Examples
It's a bit like the law requiring goods to be 'fit for their purpose'. A TV has to receive broadcast signals, a kettle has to hold and heat up water, an intelligence test has to measure intelligence and a counsellor aptitude scale has to measure a person's aptitude for being a counsellor. If they don't do what they claim to do they are not valid measures. A kettle is not a kettle if you can't boil water in it and a test isn't a counsellor aptitude scale if it doesn't measure my aptitude for being a counsellor.

Validity is measured on a scale from 0 to 1:

```
0 ------------- LOW ---------------- HIGH --------------- 1
No              VALIDITY            VALIDITY            Complete
Validity        Doesn't measure     Does measure        Validity
                what it claims.     what it claims.
                Isn't fit for it's  Is fit for it's
                purpose.            purpose.
```

There are four main *types* of validity:

1. Surface or Face Validity:

Definition
Where the validity of the measure is judged simply on whether it seems to be or looks appropriate. This is a very rough and ready test of validity.

Examples
As consumers we all know that you can't judge the fitness for purpose of a household appliance just by looking at it. The same applies to measurements in social science research. Face validity is useful, however, for eliminating things that are real no-hopers from the start. A kettle with no spout for example or a counsellor aptitude scale that asked me what I had for breakfast, what colour my eyes were and my inside leg measurement may be judged by some as having low face validity.

2. Concurrent Validity:

Definition
Where we compare our measure with another measure of the same thing taken at the same time.

Examples
We might check to see if the potatoes are cooked by measuring the time they have been boiling, but we could get a concurrent measure of validity by sticking a fork into them as well. Let's say we want to measure staff attitudes to the counselling service in an FE

College, so we give a questionnaire to all staff and to estimate the validity of the measure (Is it really tapping into staff attitudes?) we might compare the results with the number of referrals from staff. Staff may say that they support the counselling service, but their behaviour as referrers may not support this. Our questionnaire would then have low validity.

3. Predictive Validity:

Definition

Here we are assessing validity by trying to relate our measure to some future event, to see if it can predict a certain outcome that we would normally associate with high validity. Sometimes we may be using a measure specifically to act as a predictor - like forecasting the weather by looking at seaweed and pine cones.

Examples

Staying with the weather example, you may know that there are some 'old fashioned' methods of forecasting the weather using natural objects. Some people reckon that when the pine cones open we're in for a dry spell. Let's suppose that we wanted to estimate the validity of using pine cones as predictors of the weather. We could measure the degree of openness of the pine cones by using a ruler (our measure), then note the weather changes over the next few days (the future event) and estimate how high the validity of pine cone forecasting is.

If we have long waiting lists at a counselling agency, we might want to devise a test to give to prospective clients to screen them so that we only accept those who will definitely benefit from counselling. We would give the test to all prospective clients and then compare the clients' results with follow-up measures which tell us how much benefit the clients got from the counselling sessions. (We would first have to establish the validity of the measures we used to test the benefit gained from counselling!)

4. Construct Validity:

Definition

This is a form of validity which is usually of interest only to those engaged in high-level research. It is an attempt see how far the theoretical notion (construct) on which we've based our measure is what it says it is.

Suppose a deodorant manufacturer claims that their product will increase your personal magnetism. Is this claim valid, we might ask? In the first instance, validity here hinges upon the existence (validity) of the notion (construct) of 'personal magnetism'. What do you think? Does personal magnetism exist, or not? Social science is littered with such notions that have no basis other than that established by construct validity. Intelligence is probably the best-known example. Think of an idea or notion in counselling theory and you could try to establish the validity of it. How about empathy, congruence and non-judgmental warmth to name but three?

The actual process of establishing the validity of a construct is rather complicated and involves advanced statistical procedures, so I won't go into detail here. Basically the process involves measuring lots of characteristics which you think are evidence of the main construct and comparing the measures of these subsidiary characteristics. The assumption is that the construct you are trying to validate is the one thing which links all the other measures. At this level of calculation some people find it difficult to distinguish between the lies, the damned lies and the statistics!

Reliability

Definition

Sometimes called consistency - it refers to the likelihood of getting the same results over and over again if we repeated the measure in the same circumstances. There are two main areas in social science research where reliability is important, one where the reliability of an observation or observer is at issue. The second is where the reliability of the measuring device itself is at issue.

1. Inter-Observer Reliability:
Definition
When two or more observers agree on what they've observed (high inter-observer reliability).

Everyday Example
So that teachers can be fair in their allocation of marks they often 'cross-mark' assignments. This is where two or more teachers mark the same piece of work and compare marks to make sure that they are working to the same standard.

Research Example
Let's say two colleagues wish to rate the performance of another counsellor colleague in a particular session. They videotape the session and sit down to watch it, rating scales in hand. When it's over, they compare notes - if their ratings agree or are very close, then there is high inter-observer reliability. If they disagree and their ratings are very different, there is low inter-observer reliability. In a research setting, it's important to obtain high inter-observer reliability and this is usually achieved by training the observers in the proper and consistent use of the rating scale. It is not uncommon for *many* observers to be used in a piece of serious research since this should increase the inter-observer reliability. Can you work out why? (The answer is in Chapter 4 called 'Distributions - Samples and Populations'.)

2. Reliability of a measure:
There are three ways of estimating this depending upon the type of measure you're using. Two of these ways are only really important if you're devising a psychometric test and since I don't think we'll be getting on to that in this book, I'll simply describe:

Test - Retest Reliability
Definition
This is simply the taking of repeated measurements. Results that are similar indicate a reliable measure, whereas wildly different results indicate an unreliable measure.

Everyday Example
Measuring the same thing twice is the most commonly used everyday method of checking reliability. In physics at school I was taught to measure everything three times and take the average of the three measures. Whilst this isn't necessary for most everyday measures, I still find that measuring something twice prevents me from making simple mistakes such as misreading the tape measure.

Research Example
It is common practice to make sure that any test or questionnaire you devise, however simple, is reliable. The most simple method is to give it to a small group of people twice with a week or so gap in-between. Agreement between the test and the re-test results means high reliability. Big differences between the test and re-test results means low reliability.

Note Whilst validity and reliability are most often thought to tell us something about the *measure*, we have come to appreciate that in all areas of science, they can also be telling us something about the *measurer* and I'm not simply referring to inter-observer reliability. The most accurate and sensitive measuring device can be rendered useless in the hands of someone who doesn't know how to use it properly. There will be more on this in Chapter 6 called 'Research Methods'.

Correlation
Both reliability and validity depand upon a statistical procedure called correlation. It is based on the idea that two things may be associated or co-related, i.e.

• my weight *increases* as I eat *more* food, or

• the amount of petrol in my car's fuel tank *goes down* as I drive *more* miles.

We cover this procedure in more detail in Chapter 6 'Research Methods', but for now it is just necessary to know that
> * in the case of validity, for example, correlation means that the more open the pine cones are, the less it rains, (predictive validity) and
> * in the case of reliability, for example, correlation means that the same people getting a high score on my counselling aptitude scale on Monday, also get a high score when I give them the test on the following Friday (test-retest reliability).

Great care must be taken when using correlation, since it can't tell us anything about cause and effect relationships. It just tells us that as one thing varies, so another thing varies in a consistent way. Chapter 6 covers this and other issues regarding correlation in much more detail.

Test yourself on Chapter 2 with these questions:

1. Which scales of measurement are the following examples of?
> a) The number of miles driven by Community Psychiatric Nurses in 1992.
> b) Categorising counselling services by theoretical orientation.
> c) Listing the workshops at last year's BAC Conference in order of popularity.

2. What is 'inter-observer reliability' and how would you measure it?

3. Define 'face validity' and 'predictive validity'.

Discussion Point:

Are 'empathy', 'congruence' and 'non-judgemental warmth' valid constructs? Can you think of a way of developing a method(s) of measuring them? How would you test its(their) reliability?

3 Using Numbers to Describe Things

It is not enough to measure and count accurately, reliably and validly. We have to make sure that other people can understand our measurements. This means presenting them in a clear and concise form, often having to summarise them so that they can be taken in at a glance.

When we have finished measuring and counting, we are left with what's known as **raw data**. It's called raw data for a fairly obvious reason, like a raw diamond, its value can't be appreciated until we've treated it in some way. There's just too much to be taken in and it's more than likely all jumbled up. So in order to appreciate a raw diamond it is cleaned to reveal its true form and cut into a pleasing shape in sympathy with its natural structure so as to enhance its inherent beauty. We do the same with raw data. We have to 'clean it up' using treatments which work with, rather than against, the trends in the data. We have to try to reveal the true form of the data and if possible enhance the subtle messages buried under the apparently chaotic surface.

This chapter is all about that first stage of the 'clean up' where we are trying to see the true shape of the data. The techniques are all very basic and you may well be familiar with some if not all of them. However, what I will try to do is explain why we use certain ways of describing and summarising data under different circumstances. In order to understand this you will have to read and understand Chapter 2 'Measuring Things' since all of the explanations hinge upon the type of measurements we've made, i.e. nominal, ordinal, interval or ratio.

Numbers by Pictures: Summarising and Describing Results in Pictures

The first thing to do in order to see the shape of data is to arrange it in some sort of 'picture'. The simplest sort of picture is a table.

> **Help!** If the thought of drawing tables and graphs sends shivers up your spine, turn to Appendix II called The "Rules" of Graphing - A Quick Summary', then return to this section.

1. Tables

Tabulating numbers is a very old and very simple procedure. It means taking the dozens of scraps of paper on which you've written your measurements and summarising them in one place. Suppose we want to look at the use of a counselling agency in 1992. We collect the figures from each counsellor and summarise them in the table below:

COUNSELLOR	NUMBER OF CLIENTS IN 1992		
	FEMALE	MALE	TOTAL
1	54	12	66
2	12	14	26
3	32	42	74
4	38	19	57
5	50	21	71
TOTALS	**186**	**108**	**294**

Table 3.1 Number of clients using counselling agency in 1992.

Now, with a quick glance at the table we can learn several pieces of information and with a longer look come to understand some of the possible workings of the service. We may ask questions about the data - why does *Counsellor 2* have fewer clients? Why does *Counsellor 1* have so many female clients and so few male clients?

Of course it would occur to most of us to do it like this and now we can see that there are some further pieces of information we could have included to aid understanding. We could have added to the same table some information about the time the counsellor spent working for the agency (full-time or part-time) and the counsellor's gender (male or female).

COUNSELLOR	M/F	FT/PT
1	F	FT
2	M	PT
3	M	FT
4	M	FT
5	F	FT

Table 3.2 Counsellor gender and status at counselling agency.

Clearly, even this doesn't answer all of the questions that we might have, indeed, we may have to tabulate more data about the counselling agency in order to answer more questions, or we may never be able to answer all questions with simple tables. At this stage the message is simple - don't overlook the humble table as a method of expressing your results.

2. Charts, Graphs and Histograms
Even more pictorial methods of displaying summarised data are increasingly employed to make the information more accessible. There are essentially two types of data which we can collect (see Chapter 2 'Measuring Things'):

1. **Frequency Data** : This is where we have *counted* things in categories.

• For this we use pie charts, bar charts (histograms) and frequency distributions or polygons.

2. **Other Data** : Here we have *measured* something, e.g. time.

• For this we use data curves or graphs.

3. **Correlation Data** : Measuring two variables and seeing how they are related.

• For this we use scattergrams which will be covered in the section on **Correlation** on page 118 of Chapter 6.

1. Frequency Data
Counting can only be represented by illustrating how the frequencies of occurrence of events in the various categories are distributed amongst those categories. Frequency distributions are very important graphical representations in statistics as we shall see in later chapters. Let's say that we want to look at the effects of counselling people with drug abuse problems. We decide to follow up a month's worth of clients at a particular agency for a year and look at the number of drug free months since the end of counselling for the cohort of clients in question. We collect the results and summarise them in a table.

116 clients finished the counselling programme at the agency in September 1991, all of whom were followed up each month until August 1992 to see if they were still drug-free (a pre-condition of joining the agency counselling programme). So in September there were 116 drug-free clients and as each month went by, the number of ex-clients returning to drug-taking increased. They were recorded by making a down stroke for each client per month in groups of five with the fifth client being represented by a diagonal stroke (column 2). These tallies were totalled for each month in column 3 and subtracted from 116 as each month went by as follows:

MONTH	TALLIES	NUMBER OF EX-CLIENTS RETURNING TO DRUGS	NUMBER OF EX-CLIENTS REMAINING DRUG FREE
1		0	116
2		0	116
3	II	2	114
4	I	1	113
5	III	3	110
6	IIII II	7	103
7	IIII IIII II	12	91
8	IIII IIII IIII	15	76
9	IIII IIII IIII	14	62
10	IIII IIII	10	52
11	IIII II	7	45
12	III	3	42

Table 3.3 Number of clients returning to drugs
and remaining drug free by month from
September 1991 to August 1992.

We must now decide which measure (the number of ex-clients returning to drugs, or the number of ex-clients remaining drug-free) to use. There is no set procedure here, you must decide for yourself which best fits the purpose of the research and this is a matter of opinion. It's more common in statistics to use the former, because it helps us see the shape of the distribution of the frequencies more easily. So first, I'll show what the number returning to drugs per month distribution looks like and I will be explaining this shape in much more detail in Chapter 4 'Distributions - Samples and Populations'. Next, I'll use the numbers remaining drug-free. This will give you a chance to see both ways of representing the results. This second method of counting (numbers remaining drug free) is called *cumulative* because the additions (or in this case subtractions) *accumulate* and we work with the running totals.

So we now turn the above table on its side to make frequency the horizontal axis and the categories on the vertical axis and for each column of frequencies (1 and 2) plot the frequencies against the month on a separate chart. If we draw a line linking each point we have for column 1 (number returning to drugs per month):

Frequency Polygon

Again, drawing a line linking each point for column 2 (number remaining drug-free per month):

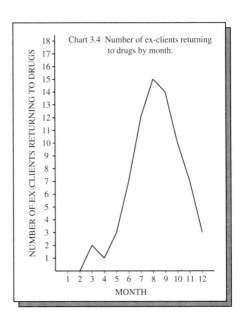

Chart 3.4 Number of ex-clients returning to drugs by month.

Cumulative Frequency Polygon

If we draw vertical bars to represent the numbers in each category instead of drawing lines to join them together, we have a bar chart or histogram:

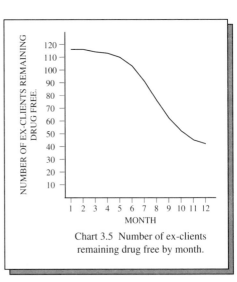

Chart 3.5 Number of ex-clients remaining drug free by month.

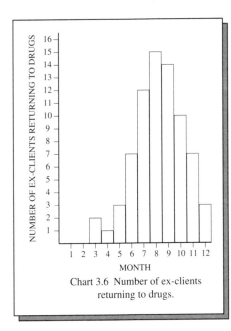

Chart 3.6 Number of ex-clients
returning to drugs.

Bar Chart or Histogram

Cumulative Bar Chart or Histogram

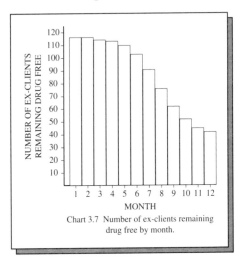

Chart 3.7 Number of ex-clients remaining
drug free by month.

Although we could use the above data to draw a pie chart, it would be less useful than a histogram or frequency polygon. (We'll learn why in Chapter 4 'Distributions - Samples and Populations'.) Instead, I'll use some different, nominal data to illustrate the best use of a pie chart. Suppose our College Counselling Service wants to report its activities to the Academic Board. We want to show how much students from each of the five faculties used the counselling service in 1992. Our tabulated data as follows can translated into a pie chart by using the calculation below (you need a protractor to draw the segments in degrees, or use our 'All Purpose Pie Chart' in Appendix II).

Pie Chart

FACULTY	No of CLIENTS (X)		DEGREES
Engineering	14		27
Pure Science	19	$\dfrac{X \times 360}{\Sigma X} =$	36
Arts & Humanities	75		142
Social Science	60		113
Business Studies	22		42
ΣX Total	190		360

Table 3.8 Number of clients attending the college counselling service by faculty in 1992.

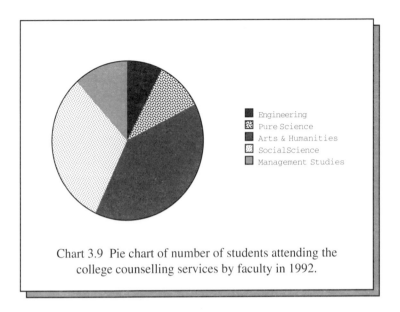

Chart 3.9 Pie chart of number of students attending the
college counselling services by faculty in 1992.

2. Other Data

Measurements (as opposed to frequency counts) are represented
graphically on **data curves**. A counsellor trainer might be
interested in looking at the improvement in skills ratings of her
trainees on a nine point scale over the period of a year-long course.
Three trainees agreed to take part and submitted tape-recordings of
their work with clients every month for ten months. The tapes were
rated by the trainer and recorded in the following table:

	SKILLS/TAPE RATING									
TRAINEE	SEP	OCT	NOV	DEC	JAN	FEB	MAR	APR	MAY	JUN
1	6	5	7	7	6	6	5	4	3	3
2	5	5	5	5	4	4	3	3	2	2
3	7	7	6	6	5	5	5	4	4	3

Table 3.10 Skills rating of trainees by month.
Skills rating scale from 9 (low) to 1 (high).

The results were represented graphically by using ratings on the vertical axis and time in months on the horizontal axis. Note that the vertical axis scale has been 'turned upside-down'. This is because an improvement in the trainees' performance is indicated by a *lower score*, so that we can see on the graph an improvement is indicated by *upward* movement. All three trainees' ratings are drawn on the same graph:

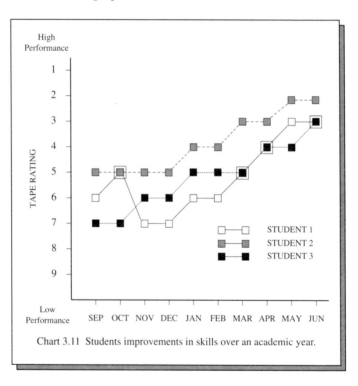

Chart 3.11 Students improvements in skills over an academic year.

It is sometimes very helpful to draw several sets of data on the same set of axes, since it allows the reader to quickly appreciate any trends in the data or values around which many performances cluster. This tendency for results to group around certain values is called *central tendency* and is covered more fully in the next section. Before we move on to the next section, if you're not familiar with drawing graphs or *graphing* as statisticians say, read

Appendix II called 'The "Rules" of Graphing - A Quick Summary'. It should help get you on the right track.

Descriptive Statistics - Summarising and Describing Results in Numbers

If, as is often the case, we have a large number of measurements, it is sometimes not possible to present a visual picture until we have done some numerical summarising first. This is not difficult at all, in fact most people do it instinctively when they say 'on average'. The 'average' is only one of the features of sets of scores that it is useful to know.

Everyday Example
When I was at school, we would often have class tests in each subject. When the results were read out there were four things I wanted to know. The first was my own score. I would often fantasise getting 80 or 90 out of 100. I also had a nightmare where I got 90 out of 100 only to discover that everyone else had scored higher than 90! So the second piece of information I required was, the (roughly) average score. I could then place myself somewhere in relation to the average. This was still not enough, because I wanted to know by how much I had missed the top mark (so I needed to know that too) and by how much I had escaped the indignity of bottom of the class (and that was my last piece of essential information).

So in order to really understand how well I had done, I wanted to know:

My score.
The average score.
The top score.
The bottom score.

These four features of a set of data are essential for statistical analysis also. Knowledge of these four features plus the number of scores (i.e. the number in the class) allows us to do some very powerful calculations and make some powerful assumptions about the data. Statisticians would use the following terms:

Average = *Measure of Central Tendency* of the scores.
Top score and bottom score = *Measure of Dispersion or Spread* of the scores.

1. Measures of Central Tendency

An 'average' is a measure of central tendency - the extent to which a set of scores group around a mid-point. Statisticians have devised measures of central tendency that can be used with each of the scales of measurement.

Mode

The mode is the most frequently occurring value in a set of scores, the most 'popular' so to speak. It can be found (hardly 'calculated') by simply looking at the data. If there are only a few scores, the mode is not a very useful measure of central tendency. It is, however, often quoted for large samples. If a histogram or frequency polygon is plotted, the mode is the peak of the histogram or polygon.

A group of seven counsellors decides to see to what degree they agree on standards of counselling. They watch a videotaped counselling session and rate it individually on a nine point scale, where 1 is an excellent performance, 9 is a poor non-therapeutic performance and 5 (the mid-point) is minimally therapeutic. Their ratings are as follows:

COUNSELLOR	RATING
1	3
2	4
3	2
4	4
5	3
6	5
7	4

Table 3.12 Audiotape ratings by seven different counsellors.

The mode (modal rating) is 4 (the most frequent rating)

Advantages:
• It is the only measure of central tendency that can be used with nominal data.
• It is very simple to calculate especially with large sets of scores.
• Is very useful with sets of scores that do not have a symmetrical distribution. (More about this later in the chapter.)

Disadvantages:
• It is not a very powerful measure - it can't be used in further calculations and if you use it with any data that is more than nominal, you are leaving a lot of the information contained in the data untapped.
• There may be more than one mode in any set of scores. Such sets or distributions of scores are called bimodal (two modes) or multimodal (many modes).

Median
The median is defined as the value that has as many scores above it as below it, the 'middle' score so to speak.   The median score is the middle score. So if, as above, 7 counsellors rate the same video tape of a counselling session on a nine-point scale as follows:

2,3,3,4,4,4,5   median = middle score (2,3,3, 4, 4,4,5) = 4

If we have an even number of scores, then the median is the point halfway between the two middle scores (the average of the two middle scores) after putting all the scores in rank order. An eighth counsellor turns up to rate the tape so the median is now:

2,3,3, 3,4, 4,4,5   median = (3+4)/2 = 3.5
also note that the set of scores now has two modes, 3 and 4

Advantages:
• It is a measure of central tendency purpose-built for use with ordinal data. (You can use the mode, but the median is almost as

easy to calculate and uses more information inherent in the data than the mode.)

• It is easy to calculate even with large sets of scores.

• Is also very useful with asymmetrically distributed sets of scores. (Again, more about this later in the chapter.)

Disadvantages:

• It's not the most powerful measure of central tendency since it has only limited use in further calculations and if you try to use it with interval or ratio data you will be under-using the information contained within the data.

> **Help!** If you feel a bit shaky about doing calculations with formulae", take a moment to refresh your arithmetic by turning to Appendix I called "Sums - A Quick Refresher". Then return to this section.

Arithmetic Mean

This is a commonly used measure of central tendency which is usually called the 'average' in everyday language. It is calculated by adding together every score and dividing by the number of scores:

$$\text{Mean} = \frac{\text{total of all scores}}{\text{number of scores}}$$

This can be represented as a mathematical formula using symbols that represent the words used above. It's a good idea to learn the symbols used in statistics since it saves a lot of time by cutting down on the large number of words required to explain simplenumerical ideas. So here are some symbols used pretty universally in statistics. I'll use them throughout the rest of this book and you'll find them in other books too.

X =Scores in general or any score in the set.

$\overline{X}$ = The Mean Score.

If you use A B C or any letter to denote the scores, then putting a bar over the letter indicates that this is the mean value. (i.e. If the scores are A_1.....A_{12} then $\overline{A}$ is the mean of all the A's.)

Σ = The sum of (whatever follows).

So Σ A = The sum of all the A's.

N = The number of scores in the set.

The mean has a formula using these symbols as follows:

MEAN FORMULA

$$\overline{X} = \frac{\Sigma X}{N} = \frac{\text{The sum of all the X's}}{\text{The number of X's}}$$

So for the scores given in the above example for the median, the mean is:

$$\overline{X} = \frac{2+3+3+3+4+4+5+5}{8} = \frac{29}{8} = 3.625$$

Advantages
• The mean is the most powerful measure of central tendency, it can be used in the most advanced calculations.
• It can be used with interval and ratio data.
• It uses all of the information in the data.

Disadvantages
• Takes a while to calculate (and you can make mistakes!).
• Is very sensitive to extreme scores and is 'pulled' away from the centre of the scores in asymmetrical distributions. (More about this next.)

Next we need to look at the effects of the shape of the distribution of the scores on the measures of central tendency. It's all very well and good talking about central tendency or where the bulk of the scores lie as if such a quality could be measured reliably. However, the truth is that central tendency is as its name suggests, a *tendency*, and as such may be slightly different depending upon the method of measurement. This is never more true than when we have a set of scores that is not distributed evenly about its mid-point. Distributions like this are asymmetrical - the first half of the distribution is not the same shape as the second half. (There are some symmetrical distributions that cause problems too - bimodal or multimodal ones, but they are rare and nearly always explain themselves.)

Suppose we gave a 'counselling aptitude test' to two successive intakes of trainees on a counselling training programme. Look at the histograms drawn from the two sets of scores:

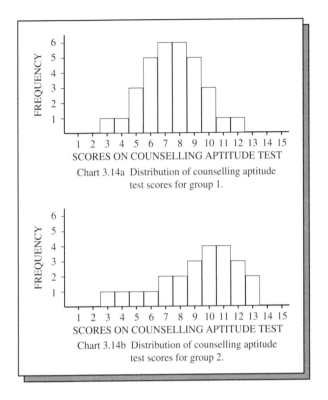

Chart 3.14a Distribution of counselling aptitude
test scores for group 1.

Chart 3.14b Distribution of counselling aptitude
test scores for group 2.

The first set is distributed symmetrically about its mid point, the second set is distributed asymmetrically. This lack of symmetry in a distribution of scores is called *skew* and can be either positive or negative. A positively skewed distribution is bunched up towards the left with a longer tail to the right. A negatively skewed distribution is the other way round - bunched up to the right with a longer tail to the left.

Whilst skew in a distribution is caused by many things, one thing can be relied upon - it exerts varying degrees of 'pull' on the different measures of central tendency. The mode is affected least by skew, the mean is affected most as follows:

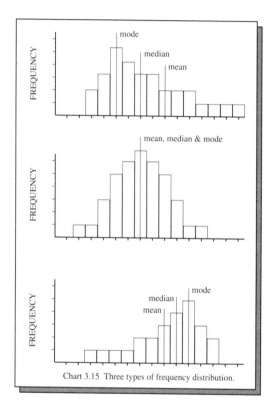

Chart 3.15 Three types of frequency distribution.

This feature helps us in two ways:

• If you know your distribution is skewed, don't use the mean - it's the least accurate measure of where the bulk of the scores lies in these circumstances.

• If you want to quickly find out whether you've got a skewed or symmetrical distribution, you don't have to draw it out - just work out the mean, median and mode. If they lie fairly close together, in no particular order, you've most likely got a symmetrical distribution. If they are spread out in the order mode, median, mean (or the reverse) then you've most likely got a skewed distribution.

You may well be saying to yourself - "So what if I have a symmetrical or skewed distribution, what difference does it make?" The answer is that skew in itself doesn't mean much. But you should remember that the numbers we collect are *always* telling us something - they may, of course, be simply telling us that we've collected a rather ordinary, unremarkable set of numbers. This is generally good news since generally speaking, the more ordinary the distribution, the more powerful statistical procedures we can use. More of this in the next chapter. Skew is a feature of distributions of scores which has ramifications for the statistics we can use, but we don't have to trouble ourselves with that in this book.

2. Measures of Spread or Dispersion.

The degree to which a group of scores is bunched up or spread out around a mid-point is an important piece of information about measurements. It tells us by how much the scores vary from each other or from the mean (or what the variability is in the scores). This is sometimes talked of in terms of the degree to which scores deviate from the mid point.

Example
Again, staying with the example used earlier on page 46 of the eight counsellors who rated the same videotaped counselling session. Lets suppose that in addition, a group of eight counselling course students also rated the tape. Here are the results of both 'teams' of raters, the qualified counsellors and the students and the histograms of the two sets of scores:

Counsellors' Ratings: 3, 4, 2, 4, 3, 5, 4, 3
Students' Ratings: 4, 3, 1, 5, 7, 4, 2, 8

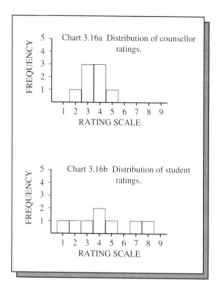

Now as you can see, the 'speadoutness' or *dispersion* of the two groups is markedly different. The counsellors' scores are bunched up around the mean, whereas the students' scores are more spread out or more *dispersed.* Another way of saying this is to say that there is more variation in the students' scores or more *variability.* Yet another way of saying the same thing is to say that the students' scores deviate more from the mid point.

So if the measure of central tendency is where the bulk of the scores lies, then scores can be closer or further away from the measure of central tendency used. The different ways of saying this can be summarised as follows:

When scores are **closer** to the mid point of the distribution:	When scores are **further away** from the mid point of the distribution:
They look **bunched up**.	They look **spread out**.
They are **less dispersed**.	They are **more dispersed.**
They have **less variation**.	They have **more variation.**
The **deviate little** from the mid point.	They **deviate a lot** from the mid point.

There are a number of ways to express or describe the degree to which the scores in a distribution are dispersed. Some of these methods involve calculations which are more complicated than the mean and pie chart formulae earlier in the chapter. If the thought of more complicated calculations makes you break out into a cold sweat, try reading Appendix I called 'Sums - A Quick Refresher', then come back to this chapter. The most simple way of describing the dispersion of a set of scores is the **range**.

Range

The range is the difference between the highest score and the lowest score. The following marks in a counselling psychology exam were achieved by students on a certain course in subsequent years and placed in rank order from the lowest to the highest:

1990/1 39, 39, 45, 50, 52, 56, 56, 65, 67, 71, 75, 81   MEAN = 58

1991/2 46, 48, 48, 51, 54, 56, 56, 62, 67, 68, 68, 72   MEAN = 58

By a coincidence the marks in the exam show that the mean exam mark was the same in both years. Is this the end of the story that the numbers can tell us? Let's calculate the range to find out what the dispersion is. This is easily done since the marks are in rank order (although this isn't necessary when working out the range, it does help avoid silly mistakes):

RANGE = Difference between the highest score and the lowest score.

1990/1 RANGE = 81 - 39 = 42

1992/3 RANGE = 72 - 46 = 26

As you can see, there is a big difference between the ranges. This tells us that the marks in 1990/1 were more dispersed or spread out than the marks in 1991/2. If there is a pass mark of 45% and a distinction gained at 75% then the range has quite an important effect on how these marks are viewed. In 1990/1 two people failed yet there were two distinctions awarded. In 1991/2 there were no fails and no distinctions, everyone was more 'average'. The tutors on the course might want to try to explain this by looking at the way they selected the students at the beginning of the course or whether the teaching differed from year to year or whether the examinations were equally hard. What do *you* make of these results?

Easy and useful though it is, the range has a severe drawback. Since it only takes into account the two most extreme scores, it cannot give a good description of a distribution that has a single extreme score sticking out at one end:

2, 2, 3, 4, 4, 4, 5, 7, 8, 72   RANGE = 70

The range of 70 for the above set of scores is, to say the least, misleading!

Advantages
•The range is quick and easy to work out.
• For rough-and-ready appreciation of results it's fine.

Disadvantages
• It's not very powerful, i.e. it doesn't use all of the information in the data.
• It can't be used in more complex calculations.
• Its loses its usefulness when a distribution is skewed or has one extreme score.

The Road to The Standard Deviation
The standard deviation is the most useful and probably the most frequently used measure of dispersion. It is powerful and with a calculator, quite easy to work out. It's also not too difficult to understand the idea behind it as long as we follow the logic. Along the way to understanding the rationale, we can learn the reasoning behind two other less useful and less often used measures of dispersion, the **mean deviation** and the **variance**. I'm not going to show you how to calculate the mean deviation here because quite

frankly, hardly anyone ever uses it, but it's useful to know what it means so that you can understand the standard deviation.

Mean Deviation
The mean deviation is short for 'mean deviation from the mean' which sounds complicated but is a very simple idea, and the idea is this: Since we are trying to measure dispersion, we take a fixed point in the middle of the scores (the mean) and measure the deviation of each score from it then calculate the mean of all of these deviations.

Now it won't have escaped those budding mathematicians amongst you, that some scores lie above the mean and some scores lie below the mean. The mean of a set of scores is like a fulcrum, it is the point at which the distribution balances so that there is just as much of the distribution above the mean as below it. So, yes you've guessed it, if we calculate the mean deviation as described above it will be zero because the deviations below the mean will be negative and will perfectly cancel out the positive deviations above it.

In order to solve this problem, the mathematicians used the fact that since if you multiply two like signs together you always get a positive, why not use the squared deviations (they'll always be positive) before calculating the mean of them?

Variance
That's exactly what the variance is. The mean of the squared deviations from the mean. The formula is as follows:

VARIANCE FORMULA 1

$$\text{Variance} = s^2 = \frac{\Sigma (X - \overline{X})^2}{N}$$

If we tried the calculate to variance using this formula we would find it a rather laborious task. Fortunately there is an alternative formula that allows us to square each value of X as we find it, the add them together and subtract the square of the mean just once at the end.

> **Help!** Don't worry if that sounds complicated - it's much simpler to do than to say!

Don't try to calculate this yet - we'll show you a step-by-step method soon.

VARIANCE FORMULA 2

$$\text{Variance} = s^2 = \frac{\sum X^2}{N} - \overline{X}^2$$

If what we're after is a single number that expresses the dispersion of a collection of scores, the variance looks as though it might just do. Indeed it is used in many more complex calculations and summaries of data, but when we have a symmetrical distribution or better still a normal distribution (see Chapter 4 called 'Distributions - Populations and Samples') the standard deviation has that extra ingredient *standardness*.

Standard Deviation
The standard deviation (S.D.) is simply the square root of the variance. (That's why the symbol for the variance is s^2.) In maths taking the square root of a number has a stabilising effect on the number. It also, in this case, gives us a number with which we can measure the distribution, in the same units of measurement as the data we have collected. There will be more on this in the next

chapter. First, here's the formula for the S.D. and a worked example:

Standard Deviation Calculation.

COUNSELLOR	NUMBER OF SESSIONS	SESSIONS SQUARED
1	12	144
2	14	196
3	16	256
4	14	196
5	13	169
6	15	225
7	18	324
	$\Sigma X = 102$	$\Sigma X^2 = 1510$

Mean

$$\bar{X} = \frac{\Sigma X}{N} = \frac{102}{7} = 14.571$$

Variance

$$s^2 = \frac{\Sigma X^2}{N} - \bar{X}^2$$

$$= \frac{1510}{7} - 14.571^2$$

$$= 215.714 - 212.314$$

$$= 3.40$$

Standard deviation

$$s = \sqrt{3.40} = 1.84$$

Test yourself on Chapter 3 with these questions:

1. What is a histogram?

2. When would you use a pie chart?

3. Define   a) The mean
             b) The median
             c) The range
and give one advantage and one disadvantage of each.

4. What is 'dispersion'.

Discussion Point

When might you need to display your information in numerical form? In your experience, are counsellors able to express themselves accurately, concisely and authoritatively using numbers?

4 Distributions - Populations & Samples

A brief look at distributions.

The term 'distribution' has already cropped up in the previous chapter. We need to have a much deeper understanding of what a distribution of scores *is* because an understanding of certain types of distributions is at the root of understanding all statistics.

> **Help!** If you don't grasp what is to follow, don't worry. You may like to read on regardless, in the hope that it'll fall into place as you go along, or leave it for a day or two before re-reading it. If it still proves too difficult you can revert to 'cookbook mode' and no one will know the difference!

I would like to start off with an example that all readers could relate to, but no-one draws graphs in 'everyday life' so it's difficult to think of an 'everyday example'. I'll use height (as in "I'm 5ft 10ins") as my example for this section, since we all have some height and we all understand the simple issues involved. This example will also serve the purpose of introducing some of the issues behind research methods and although I'll not be making too much of that now, I'll be returning to these issues soon.

Let's say I want to find out the mean (average) height of people in Britain. 'All the people in Britain' is then the *population* I wish to measure. (I'm using the term *population* here statistically, not demographically - see later in this chapter on page 66.) There is only one way to do this and that is to measure the height of all the people in Britain then calculate the mean. Now that would clearly be impossible, or at least not worth the effort. So what should I do? A statistician would say that the best that I could do would be to estimate the mean height of people in Britain. In other words, in the absence of being able to measure the height of everyone in Britain and take the mean, I'm going to have to do something that will give me a close enough guess. How do I do this?

Most readers will know that the way to do it is to measure the height of a few British people in the hope that they are *representative* of British people in general. Then I calculate the mean of this small, hopefully representative, group with the expectation that the mean will be near enough to the national mean to suit my purpose. I will have *estimated* the national mean.

I decide to follow this procedure and so I measure the height of twenty people and calculate the mean. I also decide to represent these heights that I've collected graphically. If you've read Chapter 3 you'll know that this sort of data is best drawn as a ***histogram*** as follows:

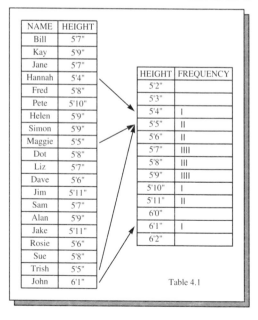

NAME	HEIGHT
Bill	5'7"
Kay	5'9"
Jane	5'7"
Hannah	5'4"
Fred	5'8"
Pete	5'10"
Helen	5'9"
Simon	5'9"
Maggie	5'5"
Dot	5'8"
Liz	5'7"
Dave	5'6"
Jim	5'11"
Sam	5'7"
Alan	5'9"
Jake	5'11"
Rosie	5'6"
Sue	5'8"
Trish	5'5"
John	6'1"

HEIGHT	FREQUENCY
5'2"	
5'3"	
5'4"	I
5'5"	II
5'6"	II
5'7"	IIII
5'8"	III
5'9"	IIII
5'10"	I
5'11"	II
6'0"	
6'1"	I
6'2"	

Table 4.1

You can see how each person's height becomes a tally in the second table, from Hannah, the shortest through Maggie and Trish up to John the tallest. This second table shows the frequency with which each height occurs within my group of twenty people. This is the way we generated Table 3.3 on page 39.

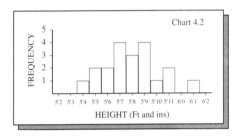

If we calculate the mean following the formula on page 49 we find that the mean height of our small group is **67.95 ins or 5ft 8ins** rounded up to the nearest inch. You could also work out the median and mode to test your knowledge.

The histogram above is called a frequency *distribution* because it is a graphical representation of how the twenty heights in my table are *distributed* across the scale of heights from 5ft 2ins to 6ft 2ins (these are just the limits I have chosen on my graph). The histogram is really made up of building blocks, each one representing one height measurement. So we can see where each of the twenty people measured actually are in the distribution as follows:

You should be able to fill in the missing names. Whenever we take a measurement and represent it in a histogram we can always 'find it' there so to speak in the same way as we can 'find' Sam's height measurement in the histogram above. This is because all of the measurements can be found in what's known as the area under the curve. We can see this in the chart below if we imagine that the mid points on the top of the bars of the histogram have been joined together to make a curve. The shaded portion is the area under the curve. The corner bits left out tend to be cancelled out by the extra corner bits included.

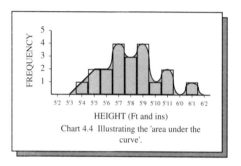

HEIGHT (Ft and ins)

Chart 4.4 Illustrating the 'area under the curve'.

For small numbers, the curve looks jagged and uneven which makes it difficult to use as an indication of the overall shape of the distribution. The term 'area under the curve' makes much more sense for large frequency distributions of hundreds of measurements. Such distributions lose their jagged edges and begin to look much more like curves. This is illustrated in Chart 4.5 below.

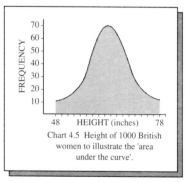

HEIGHT (inches)

Chart 4.5 Height of 1000 British women to illustrate the 'area under the curve'.

This area under the curve can be used in calculations, but it's not really necessary to understand why or how at this stage. I'm only showing it here so that you can understand how this demonstrates a further and much more useful feature of a frequency distribution, namely that since all of the measurements in a frequency distribution can be 'found' in the area under the curve, we can quickly answer questions such as "How many people are taller that 6 ft?" (Answer 1), or "How many people are shorter than Fred?" (Answer 9). This feature has only limited use in a small group, but if the small group really is *representative* of the whole population, then the proportions or percentages of people taller or shorter than a particular height, will hold true for the population also.

So if 5 out of 20 people are shorter than 5ft 7ins in our representative group (see Chart 4.3), then we can expect the same proportion of the population of Britain in general to be shorter that 5ft 7ins, i.e. one quarter of the population of Britain is shorter than 5ft 7ins. By the same token we could tell Pete, for example that he is taller than three-quarters of Britons.

A counselling-related example might be finding out how many clients are seen, on average, by a counsellor in a typical week. We could start by a taking a small group of BAC members and counting many clients they saw in a typical week. We could then draw the frequency distribution and work out the mean. If our small group was representative we could assume that our data were a close enough estimate of BAC members in general. We could then make statements about the average number of clients seen by BAC members, or that for example, 50% of BAC members see so many clients per week.

The next tasks are firstly to find out what samples and populations really are and secondly to find out just how to take a *representative* sample.

Populations and Samples

So far we've looked at the general techniques of collecting our measurements and presenting them in meaningful and attractive ways. The contexts in which the measurements are made are vitally important for three reasons:

1. As we have already learned, the context helps us understand the power of the measure (i.e. whether our measure is nominal, ordinal, interval or ratio).
2. The context helps us ensure that our measure is valid and tells us how reliable it needs to be.
3. It's the context that directs us to a particular part of the world to collect our measurements. So now it's time to ask ourselves the question "What are we collecting this information for?"

There are many reasons for collecting data, but this book will concentrate on just two rather broad purposes for data collection:

1. Taking measurements to describe one circumstance or identifiable whole group of circumstances for a report, or case study. A good example of this would be recording client numbers and demographic details for the annual report of a counselling service or agency.
2. Taking measurements so that we can make general statements about a larger group of people or circumstances than the one we have used. So, although in a study to evaluate the effects of counselling, we might have taken measures from 20 students at one particular college, we want to be able to generalise our findings to all students at that college or all students in the country.

What separates the above two examples is whether we are dealing with a **population** or a **sample**. The first example describes a population, the second a sample.

Here are the definitions and some further examples:
Population: The total number of people, objects, events or

measurements sharing one or more features.

Examples

> **People:** All of the students at Wigan and Leigh College, all of the people aged under 16 in Britain, all of the accredited counsellors in BAC.
>
> **Objects:** All of the baked beans produced by Heinz in the week beginning 11/1/93, all of the cars in Europe, all of the copies of this book.
>
> **Events:** All of the reported road accidents in Wales in 1992, all of the counselling sessions in any university counselling service ever, all of the responses I could possibly make in any counselling session ever.
>
> **Measurements:** The heights of all the people in Britain, the ages of all of the members of BAC, all of the lengths of all the pieces of string in the world.

Sample: Simply a part of a population. Any part of any population specified by the person taking the sample.

Examples

> **People:** The first 20 students that walked through the door at Wigan and Leigh College last Tuesday morning.
>
> **Objects:** The baked beans selected at random by the Heinz Quality Control Department during the week 11/1/93
>
> **Events:** The two road accidents I saw in Wales whilst on holiday in 1992.
>
> **Measurements:** The heights of the twenty people used in the example on page 62.

Some things now become obvious from the above examples:

• That populations and samples are largely what you make them. They are defined and manipulated by the researcher.

• That whilst some populations are real and finite, i.e. all of the students at Wigan and Leigh College, some are conceptual, virtual, imaginary or infinite, e.g. all of the responses I could possibly make in any counselling session ever.

• Some real populations, though finite are difficult or impossible to measure, e.g. all of the lengths of all of the pieces of string in the world.

• That there are many different ways in which we can arrive at a sample from any given population. We will look at this in some detail later in this chapter.

• Most importantly for the budding researchers amongst you, when we start seeing *possible measurements* as populations, we open up a whole new area of potential in the way we treat measurements as numbers.

When to use a population: If the population is small and discrete (well defined) then it's best to use the population, rather than a sample. So, if you are writing an annual report for a counselling service, it will be appropriate to use the population of measurements, e.g. all of the clients who used the service in the year of the report.

When to use a sample: If the population is large and difficult to access, you will have to take a representative sample and then generalise your findings to the population as a whole. So if BAC ask you to find out what their members in private practice charge then you would have to take a small sample of members to ask and generalise your findings to the whole population of members. (You can select an appropriate method of sampling when you read through the various methods later in this chapter.)

*The whole point of most research is the **generalisation** of findings from the sample to the **population** from which it is drawn.*

Help! You may want to go into 'cookbook mode' at this point if what follows confuses you even after a couple of reads-through. Join us again for the Representative Samples - what they are and how to get them' section later in this chapter.

For instance, if I define my population as all of the heights of all of the people in Britain, that means that my range of measurement goes from 0ft 0ins to very tall (it's one of those populations that it's impossible to measure). That's the population of measurements. Now any sample of heights I choose to take (like the heights of the people in my small group or *sample* of twenty on page 62) is then just a very small part of the distribution of the frequency of occurrence of the *possible heights* that people in Britain can be.

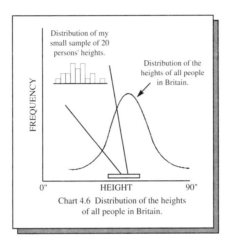

Chart 4.6 Distribution of the heights
of all people in Britain.

Chart 4.6 above illustrates this, although it would not be possible to draw it to scale - the curve for the population would go off the page! It's important to understand that the large curve is a

hypothetical distribution since we have not, cannot and never will be able to measure the heights of all the people in Britain. If you're at the "So what?" stage by now, here's the punch line.

Statistics enable us to compare our real sample average with an *imaginary* average from a population that's impossible to measure.

But only if we've taken every possible step to ensure that our sample is *representative*.

The crucial thing to understand here is:

• *That all measurements themselves belong to a population of possible measurements.*

As mentioned above, the heights of the twenty people in my small sample are just twenty examples of all of the heights that people in Britain can possibly be. It's like taking a photograph of a holiday. The photo is a snapshot, one frozen moment from all of the possible moments in that holiday. The photograph is the 'measurement', the whole holiday is the population of 'possible measurements'. So when possible measurements are themselves seen as populations of measurements, then all **real** measurements we can make in a research study become part of that huge range of possible measurements that we've defined as the population. We can have then:

• *A sample of participants in our study* (counsellors, students, clients, passers by, members of the general public or whoever), and
• *A sample of their responses or measurements taken from them* (height, counselling ability, rating on an anxiety scale, opinions about counselling or whatever).

So when we say that a sample must be representative, not only do the people I measure have to be a representative sample of people,but the measurements that they yield must be a representative sample of possible measurements. I would not, for example measure the heights of the people in my sample whilst they were standing on tip-toes or stooping. I would not measure the heights of the people in my sample with their shoes on or with different tape measures. If I didn't take such precautions I would have taken either an unrepresentative sample of heights or a representative sample of the heights of say, stooping people, which would be no use at all in my quest to estimate the mean height of people in Britain.

Representative Samples - what they are and how to get them.
A representative sample is one that contains within it all of the

essential characteristics of the population from which it is drawn in the correct proportions.

An example of this is when the pre-general election pollsters search for the Parliamentary Ward that most closely mirrors the features of the nation as a whole. They then hope that because the chosen ward contains all of the essential characteristics (those that affect voting behaviour) of the nation in the correct proportions, the result declared in the chosen ward will predict the national result.

Similarly, in our attempt to estimate the average height of Britons, we are hoping that the sample of twenty people in our study contains all of the essential characteristics (those that affect height) of the population of Britain.

How do we obtain a representative sample? Whilst it is true to say that this is not easy to get a 'cast iron guarantee' that a sample is representative, we do know that statistical procedures are quite forgiving if we fall short of perfection.

> *The aim is to be as correct as possible in our sampling procedure,* so that although we know we are not perfect, we can put ourselves beyond criticism. In other words we should be able to demonstrate that *we did the best we could given the circumstances.* How do we do this?

There are several sampling techniques that can be used in different circumstances to get the best possible sample. Our decision will be based on what we are trying to achieve in terms of:

• Validity and reliability: if we are doing a small project for a counselling course, we would not go to the same lengths as we would if we were doing Government funded research into the effectiveness of brief therapy.
• Expense and convenience: good sampling takes time and costs money. Even our Government sponsors may not want to fund our

attempts to get that perfect sample.
• The research method we are employing: surveys require different sampling methods from experimental studies.

All of the following methods can yield a representative sample given the right situation. Some are more difficult (or impossible) to do properly under some circumstances, e.g. we *couldn't* have taken a random sample of the population of Britain. A sample is unrepresentative if some error has crept in and the sample is said to be biased. Statisticians can calculate some kinds of error (random errors) quite easily and include allowances in statistical procedures for a certain amount of random error (they know that data collection is a fallible process). Researchers then try to include as many random methods in their sampling as possible, so as to take advantage of this feature of statistical tests.

Random Sampling
Description: The sample is selected by chance, with each member of the population having an equal chance of being selected.
Method: Assign a unique number to each member of the population then select numbers at random. If the population is small, write the names or numbers on paper and then draw like a raffle until the desired sample size is achieved. (See Appendix IV 'Random Number Table'.)
Example: All clients who attended the Drug Rehabilitation Counselling programme in 1992 were given a number and then 20 were drawn out of a hat to take part in a post-treatment study.

Systematic Sampling
Description: Each member of the population has an equal chance of selection, as in the random sample, but the sample is chosen systematically according to a fixed method *(or system)* rather than by chance.
Method: The members of the population fall in a natural order or are put in an order before a proportional sample is taken, e.g. 1 in every 100 (this is called the sampling ratio) then a

random starting point is chosen. The starting point is chosen at random between 1 and in this case 100.

Disadvantage: If there is some unsuspected regularity or rhythm in the order, an error or bias will be introduced.

Example: All 2,650 first year students enrolling at The University were arranged in order of age. A sample of 100 was required, so a number between 1 and 26 was chosen (19) by using a random number table (see Appendix IV). Then every 26th name was chosen from the list until 100 had been chosen, starting at number 19.

Stratified Sampling

Description: In many situations the researcher will have some knowledge of the characteristics of the population. In stratified sampling, this knowledge is put to use. Each known characteristic of the population (age, sex, ethnic origin) is a stratum from which cases are sampled.

Method: Use your knowledge of the population to look at the proportions for each stratum, e.g. 54% males, 46% females, 20% aged under 20, 34% aged between 21 and 40, 46% aged over 40. Then sample randomly from each stratum in accordance with these proportions. (This is known as a *stratified random sample.)*

Advantage: If information about the strata is accurate and the sampling is properly done, this method delivers the most representative sample with fewer possibilities of bias or error.

Example: In a survey designed to improve Counselling Service publicity, the College looked at its student population and found the following proportions in the following strata: 59% female, 41% male, 11% declared disabled, and various proportions in different ethnic minorities. The researcher then took a random sample of 200 from the 5,000 students so that 118 were women (59% of 200), 81 men and 22 were self-declared disabled and so on throughout the ethnic groups.

Cluster Sampling

Description: This relies on the existence of natural groups such as houses, blocks of flats, streets, people in a family, children in a classroom. A cluster sample is one in which a set number of cases is sampled from each cluster or naturally occurring group.

Method: Take a naturally occurring cluster that is relevant to your situation then select from it at random the number of cases you require.

Example: In order to discover attitudes towards the College Counselling Service, a sample of ten students was taken at random from each course in the college. Care must be taken to ensure that the same people cannot be chosen twice, i.e. that the course groups do not overlap.

Convenience or Opportunity Sampling

Description: Not really a bona-fide sampling method, just what most people do most of the time. It has been said that the social scientist's choice of sample is largely dictated by *convenience*. That's why so many psychology experiments are done on...psychology students. They're convenient. Much small-scale research is conducted on passers-by (because the *opportunity* was there) rather than go to the trouble of using a proper sampling technique.

Method: Choose whoever is convenient whenever you have the opportunity.

Advantages: It's cheap and should not be ignored. Nearly all sampling has an element of convenience and opportunity about it. Absolutely proper sampling is really expensive in time and money.

Disadvantages: Truly horrendous risks of bias. If you have a biased, unrepresentative sample, then you cannot generalise your results. This would render useless most research since the aim is to be able to generalise from the sample to the population.

Example: A psychologist wanted to study conformity, but to avoid the time and expense of a random sampling method she used her undergraduate psychology students. Her findings could later be criticised for telling us little about conformity in the general population because psychology undergraduates may not be representative of 'ordinary' people.

Note: The above methods can be combined in order to get the right balance between precision and convenience. As mentioned above all sampling in the real world contains an element of convenience, but most stratified, cluster and systematic samples contain an element of randomness or chance too.

Example
Do remember the example earlier in the chapter concerning how much BAC members charge? (See page 68.) What sort of sampling would you use? You would have to take the following steps:

    1. You need access to the BAC membership file. Even though BAC have asked you to do this study, you should talk over the ethical and possibly legal issues in using the membership list. (See Chapter 5 called Ethical Considerations.)

    2. There are several things you could do to protect the confidentiality of members - e.g. dealing with membership numbers rather that names.

    3. A random sample would be possible by using random number tables to select from the list of membership numbers. This would not be the best method though, because there is still a chance that your sample may be biased. For example, members in the South East may charge more than members in the North of England. Your random sample may not get the proportions of members in these geographical clusters right.

    4. Cluster sampling would be better using, for example, post codes to group members into areas. You could then take the right proportions of members from each geographical cluster at random. This would make sure that the proportions of the membership as a whole in each region were accurately

reflected in your sample.

5. You might consider getting even more sophisticated if you wanted to ensure that each Division within BAC (these would be strata) gained proportional representation in your sample. There is a problem here though because an individual member can be in more than one Division.

6. You might then decide for convenience, that your geographical clusters according to postcodes are as far as you can go, given the time and effort involved in disentangling any strata in the population from the membership list.

More on Distributions - The Normal Distribution

You may have noticed that some of the distributions illustrated in this book have the appearance of a symmetrical 'bell-shaped' curve. If you happened to be in the habit of going around getting samples of measurements of natural events in the world and plotting them as curves you would find that this bell-shaped curve kept cropping up over and over again. It seems as though this shape is a natural property of some distributions of measurements.

It is also possible to obtain this shape theoretically if we assume that the measure is derived from *many small factors acting at random.* This shape is called **The Normal Distribution curve.** It is generally assumed that the normal distribution theoretically matches the process by which things actually come about in the real world.

The normal distribution curve is important not only because it seems to describe events in the natural world, but also because it describes the distribution of probabilities that certain things might happen. It is used in this way as a *probability distribution* by statisticians as the basis for some powerful statistical procedures. Although these procedures are beyond the scope of this book, it's important to know *how* we get a normal distribution so that we can appreciate *why* we keep on seeing this shape over and over again in the data we collect and plot. Also, we will explain shortly how the standard deviation can be used to split up the normal distribution into handy standard chunks.

> **Help!** Don't give up and go into 'cookbook mode' just yet, the next bit isn't that difficult, plus we think it's really interesting and well worth the effort.

Example:
A normal distribution is what we get when a large number of random variables are influencing a measure. In order to demonstrate how this works, we'll go back to our *'height of people in Britain'* example. You may have noticed that the shape of the distributions on pages 64 and 69 follows the bell shaped normal distribution curve. This is because the distribution of heights of humans is approximately normal.

How does this come about?
• Height is determined by a whole host of factors *(or variables)* - some inherited, some as a result of upbringing, e.g.
> Inherited factors - height of your mother, height of your father, height of your maternal grandmother, height of your paternal grandmother, etc.
> Upbringing' factors - your mother's diet whilst she was pregnant, her health whilst she was pregnant, whether you were breast fed, your diet as an infant,childhood diseases, etc.
• Each one of these factors may affect your height in a positive way (make you taller), or a negative way (make you shorter).
• Each one of these factors is independent of each other - the height of your paternal grandmother does not affect your diet during infancy.
• Whether any factor has a positive effect (maybe your paternal grandfather was 6ft 6ins) or a negative effect (maybe your paternal grandfather was only 4ft 6ins) is determined by chance, i.e. at random.

• We now have all of the ingredients for a normal distribution:
   A large number of factors
   exerting a varying effect on the outcome
   each acting independently and
   each acting at random.

It is easy to show how this actually makes a normal distribution - you can do this demonstration yourself with four coins.

Let's suppose that an individual's height is determined by many factors acting at random. Each factor can be represented by a coin with an equal chance of exerting its effect in a positive way (heads) or a negative way (tails). If we limit our example to considering four factors (four coins) A, B, C, and D, then an individual's height will be the result of how many positive (heads) and how many negative factors (tails) they end up with out of four.

The tallest individual then, is one with four positive factors (heads), the shortest with four negative factors (tails) and an individual of average height has two heads and two tails.

Now we need to look at how likely it is that a given individual is going to be tall, average height or short. This is done by working out how many ways there are of arranging our four factors into tall, average, short and so on. You can follow the logic with four coins of you own if you wish.

The tallest individual is one having all four coins heads up. There is only one way of obtaining four heads.

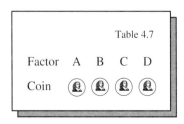

Table 4.7

Factor   A   B   C   D

Coin

Similarly there is only one way of obtaining the shortest individual - four tails.

There are, however four different ways of getting a taller than average individual with three heads and one tail, as follows:

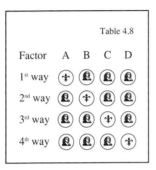

Table 4.8

Factor	A	B	C	D
1st way	✞	👤	👤	👤
2nd way	👤	✞	👤	👤
3rd way	👤	👤	✞	👤
4th way	👤	👤	👤	✞

Similarly there are four different ways of getting a shorter than average individual with three tails and one head.

There are then, following this logic, six different ways of getting two heads and two tails - the average height individual.

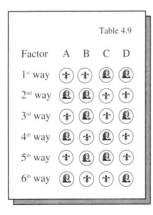

Table 4.9

Factor	A	B	C	D
1st way	✞	✞	👤	👤
2nd way	👤	👤	✞	✞
3rd way	✞	👤	✞	👤
4th way	👤	✞	👤	✞
5th way	✞	👤	👤	✞
6th way	👤	✞	✞	👤

Now if we plot these numbers of different ways against the number of heads we will have the beginnings of a normal distribution. The larger the number of variables, the smoother and more bell-shaped the curve will be - and remember a normal distribution is the result of a large number of variables acting in this way. We can see this bell-shape emerge when we use just ten variables:

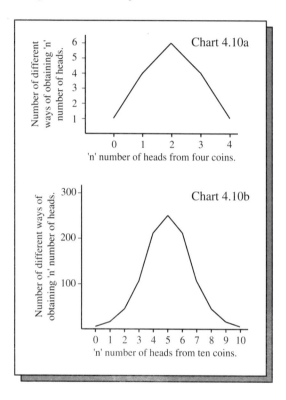

This is what is known as a *probability distribution.* We've just described the likelihood of coins landing heads or tails, i.e. the probability of four heads, three heads or two heads landing each time four coins are tossed. This distribution of probabilities is also reflected in real life. Test it if you like by taking your four coins, tossing them a few hundred times and plotting the results. There is a strong chance that your real distribution will approximate the one illustrated above.

Finally on Distributions - What Use is The Normal Distribution?

The normal distribution is a model distribution and can be treated as a template if you like, for many of the measurements that you may make even though you have not collected enough to plot a smooth curve. The rough rule of thumb is to ask yourself:

> *"Is the variable I am measuring likely to be the result of many independent factors acting at random?"*

If the answer is "Yes" then the normal distribution and its features may be of use to you.

Its main useful features are i) its symmetry and ii) the fact that the area under the normal curve (see earlier in this chapter) can be divided up in a standard way by using the standard deviation.

Symmetry: We know that the normal distribution is symmetrical about the mean - the mean divides the area under the area under the curve into two equal halves.

The Standard Deviation: The standard deviation measures off from the mean, constant proportions of the area under the curve of the normal distribution. An example will help explain this feature and how useful it is:

Example:
Staying with the example on page 75 where it was supposed that we were trying to determine how much counsellors in private practice charge per session, it would be reasonable to assume that an individual counsellor's rate of charging would be determined by many factors acting at random. So we can therefore assume that counsellors' charges in private practice are normally distributed.

Let's suppose we obtained a scale of charges from a sample of 200 counsellors then calculated the mean, median, mode, range and standard deviation, finding them to be as follows:

mean = £40
median = £40
mode = £40
range = (65 - 15) = £50
standard deviation = £8

The fact that the mean, median and mode are all the same value indicates that the distribution is symmetrical. This goes some way to confirming our assumption that it is indeed a normal distribution. If we plotted it, it may look like this:

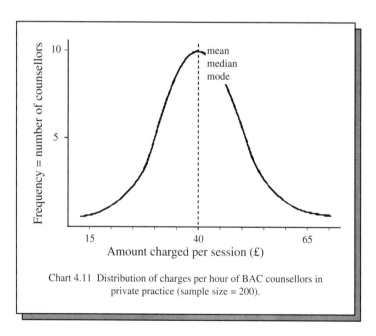

Chart 4.11 Distribution of charges per hour of BAC counsellors in private practice (sample size = 200).

Now we can see the usefulness of the standard deviation because as stated above, the standard deviation measures off constant proportions of the area under the normal curve as follows:

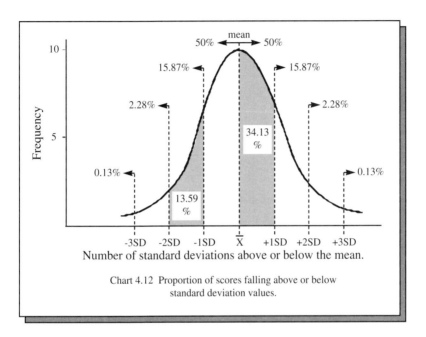

Chart 4.12 Proportion of scores falling above or below
standard deviation values.

Now whatever the values are on the axes of our distribution, whatever the measures are that we've been collecting, the proportions remain the same. So if we transpose this information onto the curve illustrated in Graph 4.11, we can see that as we measure 8 (our standard deviation as calculated above) from the mean in each direction, we can see how the proportions of the area under the curve stay the same. See overleaf.

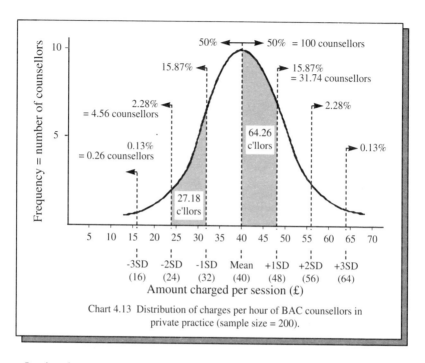

Chart 4.13 Distribution of charges per hour of BAC counsellors in private practice (sample size = 200).

In simple terms we can see that, for example,
• half of our sample charged more than £40 per session,
• if 2.28% of the area under the curve lies beyond 3 standard deviations above the mean that tells us that less than 5 counsellors in our sample charge more than £56 (2.28% of 200 is 4.56) and
• around 65 counsellors in our sample charge between £32 and £40.

The real usefulness of this feature is that we don't have to plot our scores to work this out. Since we know the rule:

> 50% of the curve above (or below) the mean,
>
> 15.87% of the curve above (or below) one standard deviation,
>
> 2.28% of the curve above (or below) two standard deviations and
>
> 0.13% of the curve above (or below) three standard deviations,

and we know the mean (40) and the SD (8), then we just count in 8's above or below the mean. So:

$$40 + 1SD(8) = 48$$
$$40 + 2SD(2x8) = 56$$
$$40 + 3SD(3x8) = 64$$

How is this useful? Well, we were careful to take a representative sample so that we could generalise to the population of counsellors in private practice in BAC in general. This means that the above proportions hold true for the whole population. Therefore if BAC had 2300 members in private practice, then we could say that around 1150 of them charge less than £40 per session or if a member of the public telephoned BAC to ask what was a reasonable amount for a counsellor to charge per hour, BAC could say that the average was £40 and that around two thirds of their members charged between £32 and £48 per session. If the caller said that they had been asked to pay £60 per session, BAC could tell them that only a very small minority of counsellors would charge that much, in fact less than 2% of their members do.

The purpose of sampling is to be able to generalise to the population from which the sample was drawn. Understanding the normal distribution and the standard deviation help us make statements about the features and proportions of the sample and population without having to go to the tedious lengths of plotting them. If you've ever tried to tabulate 200 measurements and plot them on a frequency distribution, you'll know just what a boon this feature of the normal distribution is.

Test yourself on Chapter 4 with these questions:

1. Explain the meaning of the terms 'population' and 'sample'.

2. When might you measure and write about the features of a population?

3. Why should we want samples to be representative?

4. What factors need to be present before we can assume that a measure is normally distributed?

5. What are the proportions of the normal distribution that lie above 1, 2, and 3 SD's above the mean?

Discussion Point

Given that data collection is always a balance between convenience and economy on the one hand and accuracy and validity on the other, do you think that there are corners that should never be cut in research? If so what are they?

5 Ethical Considerations

Ethics in Counselling

Some readers will be familiar with the various Codes of Ethics and Practice published by the British Association for Counselling (BAC). To date they number four; for Counsellors, Trainers, Counselling Skills and Supervision of Counsellors. In recent years, all those connected with helping and counselling have had their awareness of ethical issues raised by organisations such as BAC.

The BAC code of Ethics and Practice for Counsellors suggests that as counsellors we have responsibilities towards the client, ourselves as counsellors, colleagues and members of the caring professions and the wider community.

If you have not yet seen any of the above Codes, do obtain those that relate to your area of helping. They only cost a few pence each and are available from BAC at the address given in the Further Information' section at the end of this book.

Ethics in Research

Ethical issues arise whenever social science research is planned or carried out and however small the scale of your study or data collection, you will need to consider these. A very good pamphlet called 'Ethics in Psychological Research', written by Graham Davies, Geoff Haworth and Sue Hirschler, is published by the Association for the Teaching of Psychology (ATP) and is also available from the address given in the 'Further Information' section. The issues covered in the pamphlet are particularly applicable to research into counselling and related areas. I have used the ATP material as the basis for this section.

Data collection and research in counselling may have ethical

implications for the following:
- those participating in the study (this includes *anyone* from whom or about whom you may be collecting data),
- others they have contact with,
- members of the public,
- the researcher and
- the reputation of Counselling in general.

It is essential that the rights and welfare of the people involved are considered along with the potential value of the knowledge obtained and the need to maintain and promote a positive image of counselling. As 'Ethics in Psychological Research' says

"...research can be fun but it should not be carried out just for fun." (p. 2)

Supervision

You need to consider the following *'Four C's'* of ethical research before proceeding and if you have any doubts or uncertainties about any of them seek *supervision*. Yes, researchers have supervisors too! A research supervisor will be someone with more experience than you and may have a proven track-record in published research. Such people with a track-record in counselling or psychotherapy research may be difficult to find, so in the absence of a Counselling specialist, you could try the Social Science, Psychology or Sociology departments of your local University or College. If you are a student on a counselling course your lecturer may be able to help, or refer you to someone who can. You will need a minimum of a couple of meetings, one to outline your ideas and have them vetted and another to hear how you got on, look at your results to make sure you're treating them appropriately and check the sense behind your conclusions.

The 'Four C's' of Ethical Research

Competence
- You must work within your own limits. If you are unsure seek supervision. Seeking 'advice' is not enough since research is

ongoing and has ongoing consequences. You will, therefore, need an ongoing relationship to plan your data collection and research. This is research supervision. If you are a student you should at the very least, consult with your lecturer before proceeding.

• When conducting your study, do not claim to be more skilled or qualified than you really are. The general public are often very impressed by 'researchers'. Do not abuse this. If you are a student, say this from the outset.

Consent
• Always obtain the informed consent of the participants making sure that they fully understand what they are agreeing to, i.e. who you are, what the purpose of the study is, who (if anyone) is funding the study, what levels of confidentiality will be guaranteed.

• It is unethical to deceive people. You should emphasise sensitive aspects of the study, not cover them up. If, after supervision, you conclude that the research cannot be carried out without some deception, ask yourself if the study is really worth it.

• In all cases, participants should be debriefed afterwards so that they know what the study was about. You should be prepared to answer all questions they may ask. Participants own result should be made available to them. If this might cause distress you should not proceed. Seek supervision if the feedback at the end of a study is likely to cause distress.

• You must let participants withdraw from your study at any time (make sure they know this). You should be on the alert for any distress caused to participants and be ready to stop immediately, however inconvenient this may be to you. Remember that as a researcher, you will be in a position of influence. Do not abuse this position of power.

• If participants are not in a position to give their informed consent (possibly children, some people with psychotic illness or those with special needs), you should take special advice. In the case of children you will need the consent of the child's parent or guardian and a responsible person may need to be present or close by whilst you are conducting your study, e.g. school teacher. In the midst of all of these 'responsible' adults, don't forget to ask the child themselves.

• If you are carrying out a naturalistic observation of, for example, behaviour in public, you will not need the consent of those involved. You must, however, remember two things:

> i) Many 'public' places are in fact private properties (shopping precincts and airports) so ask permission first. (This includes permission to conduct surveys.) I remember some ill-prepared psychology students armed with camera and clipboard being carted off by security guards at Manchester Airport!

> ii) Be discreet and respect the privacy of the people you are observing. You will not want to end up with a black eye.

Confidentiality
• This should not be a novel concept to helpers and counsellors. Treat all data as confidential.

• The participants in your study should not be able to be identified.

• Keep your records safe, not where others can gain access to them.

Conduct
• Always be honest about your own competence and limitations. Do not claim to be an expert in something that you are not. Put the welfare and safety of your participants first. Do not ask participants to do anything illegal. Do not put your participants at any risk at any time. Be prepared to abandon your study.

- "You should never:
  - insult, offend or anger participants
  - make participants believe they have harmed or upset someone else
  - break the law or encourage others to do so
  - contravene the Data Protection Act
  - illegally copy tests and materials
  - make up data
  - copy other people's work
  - claim that someone else's wording is your own." p.5
  Davies, Haworth and Hirschler, 'Ethics in Psychological Research' (ATP) 1992

In conclusion and as a final reminder, if you have any doubts about any of these areas you should seek supervision before you proceed. Unethical research is worse than useless; it has harmed either people or the reputation of counselling along the way. You must always start off by asking yourself, "Should I be conducting this kind of study at all?" to be sure you can justify your study to both yourself and anyone else who may ask you.

Test yourself on Chapter 5 with these questions:

1. What are the 'four C's' of ethical research?

Discussion Point:

Over the years, many researchers in the social sciences have been tempted to conduct research that is now thought to be unethical. Do you think that some knowledge is just too important (i.e. new treatments for mental illness) to be hampered by having to keep to ethical guidelines such as consent? Do you think that there are some types of mental illness in which people cannot give their informed consent? Would you use them in your study regardless?

6 Research Methods

This book does not assume that research is only done by researchers or students with a research-based assignment to do as part of a counselling course. You may have started this book with the idea that your work situation required some data collection and report writing skills, but that research was not appropriate. If you're reading this chapter you may have changed your mind or you've become fascinated by the research side of things. We have tried to argue that counsellors should be numerate and 'research method literate' in order to claim back some lost social science territory and fight their corner, rather than be pushed to the 'counselling is just a good chat' margins of research whilst the behavioural scientists get on with the *real* business of *proving* which approaches are *effective*.

The italics in the previous sentence are there to remind us of the key words that grant-makers and fund-holders look out for when planning what services can be afforded this year. Our message is simply that research methods are here and accessible. Counsellors can go to the ball too, and if armed with a little understanding and some common-sense you will not turn into a pumpkin when midnight comes. Projects, studies, investigations, research, scientific investigations, call them what you will, all have to meet certain quality criteria before they are deemed acceptable. In order to plan and carry out an acceptable piece of work, or judge the work of others, you will need an understanding of research methods. Throughout this chapter we will refer to all studies, projects, etc. however small or grand as 'investigations' or 'studies' whichever fits best in the sentence. Please don't be either overwhelmed or insulted by the term.

In this chapter we shall be looking at the basic methods that you might employ for your investigation. You may be investigating:
• How one thing affects another thing, e.g. does the distance between the counsellor and client affect the degree to which the client likes the counsellor?

• Whether two things go together, e.g. does the self-esteem of clients increase as the number of counselling sessions increases?
• Patterns of things or events, e.g. does the non-verbal behaviour of the client change from the start of a session to the end?

Each of these investigations could require a different method of research. You may get some ideas from reading other research papers, or have done some low-key research already. This chapter will deal with the basic ways of organising an investigation:

  * Experimental Methods
  * Case Studies
  * Longitudinal and Cross-Sectional Studies
  * Correlation Techniques
  * Observational Methods (including surveys).

Each has its advantages and disadvantages, but it is necessary to understand each before deciding which is the most appropriate. We hope you're confident enough by now to be not put off by the jargon words. Whilst it's not absolutely essential that you learn them, it does make life easier when 'talking research'.

'Things' and 'People'

Before we go any further it could be an idea to stop talking about things' and introduce the term 'variables'. Simply put, a *variable* is anything that can vary, change and be measured. All the things mentioned so far in this chapter are capable of varying and being measured so they could be classed as variables.

At the same time we'll stop talking about 'people' that we might use in our investigation to collect results from and start talking about 'subjects'. Human volunteers in social science investigations are called *subjects*. How these subjects are obtained and organised will depend upon the type of investigation you are conducting, as will what you measure and how you measure it.

Hypotheses - Stating your Ideas

Before you start your investigation you must have had an idea of what you wanted to investigate and possibly of what you might expect to find. In research, the idea you have or the prediction you might make is called a hypothesis. We have looked at this notion from a slightly different angle in Chapter 1 called 'Asking Questions'. For example, you might have the idea that ingestion of alcohol affects driving ability, or you may think that clients undergoing Person Centred Therapy are more articulate than clients undergoing Play Therapy.

A hypothesis is simply a formal statement of your idea or theory in a way that allows it to be tested. In the examples above, the ideas cannot be really tested in their current form, they need to be turned into testable hypotheses. In order to do this we have to make a statement or prediction about something that is measurable. Researchers call this *operationalising*. It simply means stating something in terms of the operations or measurable events which make the 'something' in question happen. So, for example:

'Ingestion of alcohol affects driving ability' is imprecise (it doesn't say how much alcohol) and unmeasurable (how do you measure 'driving skill'?). It could however, become,

> *'There will be a difference in the number of cones knocked down on a set driving test between subjects who have drunk 4 units of alcohol and subjects who have drunk no alcohol'.*

Similarly, *'Clients undergoing Person-Centred Therapy are more articulate than clients undergoing Play Therapy'* is also unmeasurable (how do you measure how articulate someone is?). It could be written as follows:

> *Clients undergoing Person-Centred Therapy will use longer words than clients undergoing Play Therapy.'*

As you can see, the ideas have now been stated in a form in which they can be tested and a conclusion can be drawn as to their accuracy. In effect they are now hypotheses. But you might have guessed that there would be more than one type of hypothesis. In fact there are two hypotheses which we need to propose at the outset of our investigation.

Imagine that you have read your horoscope for today which suggests that 'things are going to become clearer'. Now that you have read the beginning of this chapter and fully understand the concept of operationalising statements, you may decide that your horoscope has come true. The astrologer has made a prediction (a hypothesis) and you have observed that it is correct, most probably because you believe in astrology and wanted it to be accurate. The same may be true if you were to only formulate one hypothesis for your investigation. Either consciously or unconsciously you could work to make it come true, to influence the results so that they support your hypothesis. The way to avoid this is to formulate two hypotheses that basically say the opposite of each other. The purpose of your investigation is then to obtain results that will indicate which of the two hypotheses is correct or proven.

The Null Hypothesis (a.k.a. H_0)

Help! When a psychology lecturer tried to explain the null hypothesis to me in 1970, I thought he was quite mad. It made no sense at all. You may also get a 'these people are barking mad' feeling coming over you as you read this next bit. Part of the problem is that the 'real' explanations of the null hypothesis are statistical and beyond the scope of this book. Such explanations can sound a bit silly when simplified and taken out of a statistical context. We are trying to tread the difficult line between giving enough of an explanation without going too far into statistics or making it so simple that it's incorrect. You can always go into 'cookbook mode' if the explanations seem superfluous to your needs.

The null hypothesis is the hypothesis that says that the most likely outcome of your investigation is that nothing will happen, no effect will be detected and any detectable effect will be the result of pure chance rather than anything systematic that you've done. If the null hypothesis is proved, statisticians say that the results of the investigation are 'not significant' (this will be explained later in this chapter on page 100). Examples of null hypotheses are:

*'There will be **no** difference in the number of cones knocked down on a set driving test between people who have drunk 4 units of alcohol and people who have drunk no alcohol'.*

'There will be no difference in the length of words used by clients undergoing Person-Centred Therapy and clients undergoing Play Therapy.'

At the beginning of your investigation, you will be expected to state the null hypothesis. This is just *one* of the *two* hypotheses you will have to state in order to ensure that one of them is proven. The null hypothesis is important in itself because it's the one calculable point in probability statistics, i.e. the point at which chance exerts its effect. As we move away from this 'chance' point, the likelihood that the results are due to something you've done increases until you can say with some confidence that the null hypothesis is not proven.

If the null hypothesis basically says that nothing will happen other than by chance, then the other hypothesis says that something will happen and not by chance but as a result of some systematic intervention by you the investigator.

The Alternate Hypothesis (a.k.a. H_1)
This is the other hypothesis which states that something will happen as a result of the investigation. It's the hypothesis we've looked at earlier in the chapter and just to refresh your memory, our two examples were:

'There will be a difference in the number of cones knocked down on a set driving test between people who have drunk 4 units of alcohol and people who have drunk no alcohol'.

> *Clients undergoing Person-Centred Therapy will use longer words than clients undergoing Play Therapy.'*

This alternate hypothesis is the one that is most familiar and logical to people new to research. As researchers we are looking for sufficient evidence to be able to accept or prove the alternate hypothesis. If the evidence is strong enough, statisticians would say that the results are *'significant'* (see page 100). The story doesn't end there, since to complicate matters just a little bit more, there are two types of alternate hypothesis.

1. One-Tailed Alternate Hypothesis

As we have already said, any alternate hypothesis states that there will be a significant effect, however sometimes we can say more than just that *there will be an effect*. We may have an idea about the *direction* of that effect. By direction we mean that not only would you expect there to be a difference between the length of words used by clients undergoing Person Centred Therapy and Play Therapy, but that you expect the Person-Centred Therapy clients to be the ones who use longer words. So you are predicting not just any *difference either way*, but a *specific difference*. You can say what *direction* the effect will take.

The hypothesis we've been using in our example:

> *'Clients undergoing Person-Centred Therapy will use longer words than clients undergoing Play Therapy.'*

Is an example of a **one tailed alternate hypothesis**, since it not only says that there will be a difference in the length of words used, but also that it is the person-centred therapy clients who will use longer words.

2. Two-Tailed Alternate Hypothesis

This type of hypothesis simply states that *there will be an effect and no more*. You state this sort of hypothesis when your idea or theory cannot make a prediction about the direction of any effect, i.e. whether the effect will make something specifically *more* or *less* than (or faster or slower than, etc.) something else. So we would state that there will be a difference between two things without saying which of the two things would end up bigger.

The other hypothesis that we've been using as our example:

> *'There will be a difference in the number of cones knocked down on a set driving test between people who have drunk 4 units of alcohol and people who have drunk no alcohol'.*

Is an example of a **two-tailed hypothesis**, since it predicts a difference only. It doesn't say whether the people that have drunk the alcohol will knock down more or fewer cones than those who have not drunk any.

At this point two or three questions occur to most people.

Question: *"Why are they called one and two **tailed** hypotheses?"*
Answer: Because the two extremes of a normal distribution are called the 'tails' of the distribution. The calculable statistical point at which things are caused by chance alone occurs at the centre of a particular normal distribution used by statisticians. To the left of this point lie all the probable results indicating one direction of the effect in question and to the right, results indicating the other direction of the effect. In our example using alcohol and driving skill, the point in the middle of the distribution is the point of no difference (the null hypothesis) and the two tails of the distribution indicate fewer cones knocked down by the drinkers to the left and more cones knocked down by drinkers to the right.

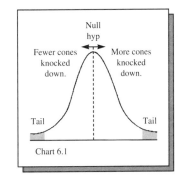

Chart 6.1

If your prediction states the direction of the effect, it is predicting that the results will be found in only one of the tails, and if you can't predict the direction, your results may be found in either of the two tails. Hence 'one' and 'two-tailed' hypotheses.

Question: "Which is better, one or two-tailed hypotheses?"
Answer: Neither is really better than the other, it just depends upon which is best suited to your investigation. If you think that your idea or theory leads you to 'know' which way your results are likely to turn out, then choose a one-tailed hypothesis. If you are not so sure, then stick to a two-tailed hypothesis. There is a statistical reason for assuming that you can be more confident in your results if you have chosen a one-tailed hypothesis. This is simply because any statistical procedure you employ only has to look in one half of the distribution illustrated above if your hypothesis is one-tailed. Any more explanation than this is beyond the scope of the present book.

Question: "Can you have a one or two-tailed *null* hypothesis?"
Answer: No. We hope this answer is obvious from the answer to the first question above. There is only one null hypothesis.

'Significant' Effects

The results of any investigation can, in statistical terms, have a quality known as 'significance'. Rather than merely looking for an effect, it is customary to look for a significant effect. If, for example, we had carried out our alcohol and driving skill investigation to find that the drivers who drank alcohol knocked over an average of 15 cones, whereas those not drinking alcohol knocked down only an average of 14. There is obviously a difference in performance, but the difference is quite small. We cannot be confident that the difference is actually due to what we did in the investigation. The difference is so small it could just as easily be due to chance. If we did the experiment again we might not find the same pattern of results. We would describe a result like this as being *non-significant*.

If the difference was larger we might be more confident that this was due to what we had done in the investigation rather than to chance factors. If we repeated the procedure we would probably obtain similar results. In this case we would describe the effect found in the results as *significant*. When we think the effect in the results is large enough to be regarded as significant we can reject the null hypothesis (which states that there will be no effect and any small effect is due to chance) and accept the alternate hypothesis. If the difference is very small then the opposite happens and we accept the null hypothesis.

Question: "How do I know when an effect is large enough to be significant?"

Answer: A very good question and one that I wish I didn't have to answer right here. This is the key to all research and frustratingly enough, the way we have planned this book, the answer lies outside our brief. Whether an effect is large enough is a statistical decision, in fact the quality we're after is called *'statistical significance'*. It is based on the likelihood or probability that the results are due to chance.

This chance factor is worked out by a statistical test (there are several to choose from covering different types of research methods) which will tell you whether the effect is large enough or not. The test will base its decision on things like the number of measurements you have taken, what scale of measurement (nominal, ordinal, etc.) you have used and what research method you have chosen. The process is a little like consulting an oracle - you ask a question ("Is my effect large enough?") and the test pronounces its decision after looking at the evidence.

Question: "Just what do you mean by 'the likelihood or probability that the results are due to chance'?"

Answer: Probability statistics is really beyond the scope of this book (see Appendix V), but to answer the question simply, it's up to you, the researcher to select a level of chance that you have faith in. Would you be satisfied that there was a 50/50 chance that your results might be due to chance? Probably not since that's only as good as tossing a coin. There are conventions to guide you - most social science researchers are satisfied with a chance of less than 1 in 20 that their results might be due to chance factors. In probability terms this is referred to as the *0.05 level of significance.*

If you want or need to take your research to the point of deciding upon the statistical significance of you results, you will have to get another book which lists and details the statistical tests that can give you the decision, i.e. the effect either is or is not large enough. (See Appendix V for information on 'An Incomplete Guide to Inferential Statistics for Counsellors'.)

You may, of course, not need or want to take the analysis of your data so far. You may be happy to use a rule of thumb or just look at the face validity of any effect you may have obtained. Whilst this may be perfectly acceptable for some applications, it is very easy to be deceived by numbers. It may be worthwhile taking your results to someone with some research experience who may be able to give you a 'ball-park' estimate. In the meantime, part of the answer is covered in the explanation of one and two tailed hypotheses on page 99. We also briefly look at statistical significance as it applies to the different research methods later in this chapter.

Experimental Method

An experiment is, in principle, a very simple thing to organise. This is true whether the subject matter is physics, chemistry, medicine or counselling. All you have to do is arrange things so that all variables are kept the same or eliminated except one. This one variable is allowed to change or, rather is *manipulated* by the researcher and the effects are observed. Then any effects can be said to be due to or caused by the changes in the manipulated variable.

Variables and the Experimental Method
The variable that we manipulate is called the *independent variable*. The variable that we measure any changes in as a result of manipulation of the independent variable is called the *dependent variable*. The variables we wish to eliminate or keep constant are called *extraneous variables*. The attempt to eliminate or keep extraneous variables constant is called *controlling* the extraneous variables.

Example: To continue our 'Does alcohol affect driving skill?' example, the *independent variable (IV)* is the amount of alcohol ingested by our subjects. We manipulate this quantity. The *dependent variable (DV)* is the number of cones knocked down (our measure of driving skill). We control *extraneous variables* by keeping the car and the driving skill course constant.

Confound it!
If we fail to control variables, they run the risk of becoming *confounded*. A confounded variable is an extraneous variable that is left free to vary in a *systematic* way, i.e. a way that makes it impossible for us to separate its effects from the effects of the independent variable. Let's suppose we had used two cars in our alcohol and driving skill study and one of the cars had faulty steering. If the faulty car was used for one condition only (it doesn't matter which one) then it would be a confounded variable. We wouldn't know whether it was the car or our manipulation of the independent variable which was responsible for any difference in performance. The use of standard control procedures (below) will eliminate or reduce this possibility.

An experiment is the only research method that can reveal a cause and effect relationship between the independent and dependant variables. There is no mystery to this, it's simply because if only one thing has changed (the IV) then it must be responsible for changes in the DV. The key to this is control. We must be sure that nothing else has changed. This turns out to be more difficult than it seems and the real skill of constructing an experiment is controlling all the relevant extraneous variables (there's no point in controlling variables which have no bearing on your subjects) without affecting the independent variable or the integrity of your measurements.

Control! Control!

The main problem in social science research is that people's behaviour is not as consistent and well ordered as the behaviour of atoms and molecules (thank goodness!). Many of the methods of control used in the social sciences have evolved to take this feature of humankind into account. The 'human factor' causes certain well-defined effects which need specific attention as follows:

1. Order Effects

Practice effect: This is where your subjects need a little time to get used to whatever procedure you are asking them to perform. So if you are asking your subjects to complete a set of problem-solving tasks, a simple solution would be to give them a couple of 'dry runs' or *practice trials* before you started recording the results. This has the further benefit of making sure they understand the experimental procedure properly.

Fatigue effect: Fairly obviously the opposite effect to practice effect where subjects' performance tails off towards the end of a series of trials.

Order effect: This is an effect which is literally caused by the order in which the conditions in your experiment occur. For example if we wished to investigate the effect of the students' gender on ratings given to their practice videotapes by counselling course tutors, there might be an order effect since we would have to show either a male tape first or a female tape first, which in itself might colour their perceptions of subsequent tapes.

Control: Order effects are controlled by either *randomising* the order of presentation of items or conditions, or *counterbalancing* - a technique where you would give half of your subjects the conditions A and B in the order AB, and the other half of your subjects would have the conditions in the order BA. These techniques distribute the order effects evenly across both (or all if there are more than two) conditions.

2. Primacy and Recency Effects

Psychologists have discovered that people can remember the first and last things in a list (names, events or whatever) much better than things in the middle. These effects are called primacy and recency. They affect our everyday lives and have an effect in experiments too. They are well well-defined types of order effect. Watch out for them in observations (you the experimenter may forget what happened in the middle of the observation) and questionnaires (subjects tending to opt for the first and last choices offered) as well as experiments.

Control: Since primacy and recency are a special type of order effect we would control for them in the same way as for other order effects, by employing randomisation or counter balancing.

3. Experimenter effects

This is an example of the 'human factor' where the experimenter themselves can affect the results in certain ways. Firstly by having expectations about the outcome of the study and unintentionally passing these on to the subjects. Secondly the experimenter's personality, demeanour and appearance can affect the results, e.g. subjects will behave differently for an officious white-coated experimenter, than they would for a laid-back, scruffily dressed experimenter.

Control: This is achieved by keeping the experimenters' personality as neutral and as constant as possible. Use only one experimenter, they should present a neutral persona and they should always use standardised instructions. Standardised instructions are written down, checked to make sure they make sense and are comprehensive, then read out to each subject.

Example:"Thank you for agreeing to take part in this study, its aim is to... I will be pleased to answer any questions you may have about the study afterwards. Can you see the equipment on the desk? When you see the red light go on, please talk into the microphone until...Do you understand the instructions? Are you ready?"

4. Demand Characteristics

When people are put in novel or unfamiliar situations they try to work out what's going on, the 'rules' of the situation if you like. These are called the demand characteristics of the situation. Subjects in experiments (or any kind of investigation for that matter) try to respond to these demand characteristics of the experiment. Human beings are not passive participants, far from it, they are trying to figure out what the experimenter wants them to do and to behave accordingly. The subjects pick up subtle clues from the experimenter.

Control: This effect wreaks havoc in medical treatment trials, e.g. where a new treatment method is being compared with a placebo. The only way to get rid of it is to do what's known as double blind trials where not only do the subjects not know what condition they're in, the experimenters don't know either. That way the experimenters can't pass on, even unwittingly, any subtle clues about the preferred outcome of the study.

5. Random Error

If you think that you've kept one step ahead of the effects listed above, you've still got to control for random errors. These are much less predictable than the systematic effects above and are less amenable to control. Random errors cannot be eliminated but they can be reduced and their effects spread evenly around all of the conditions so that they affect each subject just as much. Temperature fluctuations, lighting variations, decor, what happened on the way to the laboratory will all exert their random effect on the results.

Control: We must make sure that they don't turn into systematic variables by, for example, running all of the subjects in condition A on a bright, crisp, sunny winter morning and all subjects in condition B on a dark cold winter's afternoon. We would then have a confounded variable.

Hypotheses and The Experimental Method

Experiments are mainly looking for differences between conditions, but if you are using more than two conditions you will, in the most simple of cases, be looking for a trend. Your alternate and null hypotheses should reflect this.

Null Hypothesis: 'There will be **no** *difference* in the length of words used by clients undergoing Person-Centred Therapy and clients undergoing Play Therapy.'

Alternate Hypothesis: Clients undergoing Person-Centred Therapy will use *longer* words than clients undergoing Play Therapy.' (One-Tailed).

Or: 'There will be a *difference* in the length of words used by clients undergoing Person-Centred Therapy and clients undergoing Play Therapy.' (Two-Tailed).

If you have more than two conditions, your hypotheses should mention the fact explicitly or implicitly, by talking about increases, decreases or referring to a *trend* in the results:

Null Hypothesis: 'There will be no change in counsellor performance as the ambient noise level in the consulting room increases.'

Alternate Hypothesis: 'There will be a decrease in counsellor performance as ambient noise level in the consulting room increases.' (If you think about it, the prediction of a trend is most likely to be a one-tailed hypothesis.)

Significance and Experiments

Since experiments are looking for differences between conditions, we will talk about *significant* differences. A significant difference is one that is large enough that we are confident is not due to chance, but due to a real replicable difference. In other words if we were to take another similar sample of subjects, we would get a similar difference.

One of the main considerations in an experiment is the size of your sample (or samples) of subjects. Because the experimental method employs rigorous control of variables, you will not need as large a sample size as you would in a correlation study for example. There is a law of diminishing returns when it comes to sample size and experimentation. In most cases your effort will not be greatly rewarded if you strive for a sample size of more than twenty subjects. A large sample size is no substitute for a well-sampled group of subjects, an appropriate design and very tight control on the extraneous variables.

Organising Your Experiment

There are three basic ways of conducting experiments, the main difference being the manner in which subjects are used or allocated to the different conditions of the experiment.

Question: "Is there a limit to the number of conditions I can have in an experiment?"

Answer: In theory no, but there are practical limits. The point of having conditions in experiments is to see if there is any *difference* between them. When there are just two conditions this is relatively easy to see and test with statistical procedures. When three or more conditions are used, we would be looking for a trend in the results rather than a difference. It is possible in advanced research, to have conditions in a grid like a table, say three by three or four by four. These grids have exotic names like 'split-plots' and 'latin squares'. They are beyond the scope of this book. For now we will restrict ourselves to i) two by one (difference) designs, ii) threeor more by one (trend) designs and iii) two by two (chi-squared or association) designs. These will become clearer as we proceed through the different ways of organising an experiment.

In some cases one of the conditions will act as a control condition whereby the results obtained become a 'baseline' against which any changes in the dependent variable during the experimental condition(s) can be compared. In the alcohol and driving skill example, the no alcohol condition acts as a control. Now you have to decide which type of experimental method to use. These are called *experimental designs* and you have three basic types to choose from:

1. Repeated Measures Design
In this design, all subjects take part in all conditions of the experiment. It's called repeated measures because we repeat the measurement of the DV on the same people in both conditions. Statisticians refer to this design as *related measures* because the measurements in the different conditions are related by virtue of being taken from the same group of people. The alcohol and driving skill experiment is repeated measures.

Repeated Measures Advantages
The most obvious advantage is that this type of design gives the greatest degree of control over subject variables. As the same subjects perform in both (or more) of the conditions of the experiment, the results give a greater indication of the effect of the independent variable on their performance. For example, if a subject had poor eyesight during the no alcohol condition of the experiment, they would still have poor eyesight in the alcohol condition, similarly, if they were a nervous driver in the first condition, they would still be a nervous driver in the second - and difference in their driving ability can be more readily attributed to the effect of the alcohol. This may not be the case if different subjects were used for the two conditions of the experiment - subject variables such as eyesight, tolerance of alcohol, etc., could affect the results.

The other significant advantage of the repeated measures design, is that it requires fewer subjects. If you decide to have twenty subjects in each condition, using a repeated measures design the same twenty subjects would perform in both conditions. If a design were used which requires different subjects in the different conditions of the experiment, you would need forty subjects (twenty for each condition).

Repeated Measures Disadvantages
To refer back once again to the alcohol and driving ability example, if a repeated measures design was used, subjects would perform in both conditions of the experiment. This in itself could cause order effects, i.e. if the same driving test were to be used in both conditions, having done the test once in the first condition, they have now practised the course, and this will affect their performance in the second. It could be that they perform better because of their knowledge of the course, or they may have become tired and irritated and therefore perform worse. If they are not using their own car, they may have become used to the vehicle again improving their performance for the second condition. These are particularly associated with the repeated measures design, and they must be controlled.

One way to avoid order effects is a technique known as counterbalancing (also known as the ABBA procedure), in which half the subjects perform one condition of the experiment first (condition A), and then perform the other condition later (condition B). The other half of the subjects perform the experiment in the opposite manner (condition B then condition A). Although the subjects will all still suffer from order effects, the overall effect has been balanced out and should not affect the results of the overall group.

The other possible means of avoiding order effects is to randomise the presentation of the conditions. For the current example, the experimenter (the person conducting the experiment) would toss a coin, if it came down heads the subject would perform in the alcohol conditions first, if it came down tails then they would perform in the no alcohol condition first. This may not seem like the most scientific of methods, but when you only have two alternatives, tossing a coin is an excellent way of achieving randomisation. Another good method is pulling pieces of paper out of a hat.

In some cases it will be impossible to avoid order effects. For example, if you are comparing one therapeutic approach to another, you couldn't submit subjects to one therapy, see if they got better and then submit them to another approach and see if they showed an even greater improvement. In instances such as this, you would require different subjects for the different conditions of the experiment.

2. Matched Pairs Design
The design is basically an attempt to create a repeated measures design, but using different subjects in each of the conditions. This involves matching the subjects into pairs on the basis of variables that you consider are relevant to the experiment. Each member of the pair performs in one condition of the experiment, and the result from one member of the pair is directly compared to that of the other member. Usually, in order to conduct an experiment using a matched pairs design, potential subjects must be given a pre-test in order to find someone to match them up with. For example, you may wish to test potential subjects on a driving test and count the number of errors they make. You would then find two people who made four mistakes each and use them as a pair, another two people who made five mistakes and use them as a pair, and so on.

Matched Pairs Advantages
This design gives a reasonable degree of control over subject variables (assuming you have matched them on the appropriate variables) and, as subjects only perform in one condition of the experiment, there are no order effects to control.

Matched Pairs Disadvantages
The first disadvantage is the need to decide what variables to match the subjects on. Earlier it was suggested that you could match subjects on the basis of driving ability. However, there are other significant variables that have been ignored, such as body size, metabolic rate, age, etc., that could all affect their tolerance of alcohol, and therefore affect the results.

Even if you do decide what variables to match your subjects on (and are convinced that no-one reading your report will immediately decide that you have missed at least three important variables), there is the logistical problem of finding sufficient numbers of adequately matched subjects. This will take a great deal of time and effort, and may prove fruitless.

Many books suggest that identical twins are perfect subjects for use in a matched pairs design. Do not spend several years of your life searching for a sufficient number of identical twins. This idea is, to use a technical term, "Rubbish". For the most part you will be using adult subjects. It is highly likely that adult identical twins will have different partners, different jobs, different incomes, different experiences and different most-things, and may be no more matched than you and I.

Whilst in theory, a matched pairs design is the preferred choice if a repeated measure is not possible. In practice it is a highly difficult design to use and is not recommended.

3. Independent Groups
Quite simply, the name says it all. Different subjects perform in the different conditions of the experiment, with each subject performing in only one condition of the experiment. The two groups are independent of each other.

Independent Groups Advantages
There are no order effects and there is no need to match subjects.

Independent Groups Disadvantages
Because completely different people take part in the different
conditions of the experiment, there is a lack of control over subject
variables. If care is not taken, any difference in the results
between the conditions of the experiment may be due to the type
of subjects in each condition. For example, in deciding which
subjects perform in which condition of the experiment, if it is
simply left to the choice of the experimenter, they may (either
consciously or unconsciously) allocate subjects to the conditions
in such a way as to influence the results. It may be that the
conservatively dressed, neat and tidy, calm and respectable
looking subjects may be allocated to the no alcohol condition,
whilst the wild-eyed, boy-racer types who look as if they drive an
XR4 Turbo Egoboost are all allocated to the alcohol condition. It
may be that there is a difference in driving ability between the two
groups, but this may be due to the choice of subjects rather than
the intake of alcohol.

The way to avoid subject variables having an effect on the results
is simple. Subjects should be randomly allocated to the conditions
(again by the toss of a coin). In theory, this should give a
representative mix of subjects in each of the two conditions, and
eliminate the effect of subject variables. The other disadvantage
of the independent groups design is that more subjects are
required, but there is no easy way to solve this problem.

4. Chi-squared
This is a particular statistical test that is applied to a particular
form of independent groups design where the experimenter is
looking for the degree of association between two variables.

Example: A college counselling service asked all its clients
whether they would prefer a male or a female counsellor. The
results could be tabulated as follows in a 2 x 2 table by separating
the male clients' responses from the female clients' responses:

	Male counsellor preferred	Female counsellor preferred	Total
Male clients	32	21	53
Female clients	14	49	63
Totals	46	70	116

In a 2 x 2 association table like this we are looking for a diagonal pattern in the results to indicate an association between the two variables as indicated below:

high	low	or	low	high
low	high		high	low

Although chi-squared specifically refers to the statistical test used to tell us if we have a significant association, you do not have to perform the test. There is value in collecting and displaying data in this way since there is a striking visual impression of association when one is present.

Case Studies

Whilst most research methods require a large(ish) number of subjects, case studies provide an opportunity for far more detailed consideration of a question by restricting the number of subjects used and increasing the degree to which the individuals are studied. For example we may choose to study a therapeutic method by concentrating on two individual clients from the beginning to the end of their therapy. The report would be largely narrative, i.e. a detailed description of the progress of the therapeutic process.

Case Studies Advantages
Case studies provide us with a great amount of detailed information. They are capable of revealing and concentrating on any developmental process or the effects of a sequence of events. In a counselling setting, the subjectivity of a case study, cited as a

disadvantage below, may be seen as a distinct advantage.

Case Studies Disadvantages
As the sample size is small, generalisation to a larger population is difficult. You may have deliberately chosen subjects who were not 'typical' anyway. A second difficulty is the analysis of the results. There is not much scope for numerical analysis, but content analysis (see page 122) is a popular method of data analysis which acknowledges the various subjective viewpoints.

Longitudinal and Cross-Sectional Studies

These are two separate methods primarily concerned with looking at development over time. They approach the problem in different ways by using subjects in a different manner. To illustrate the advantages and disadvantages of both methods we will take the question "How soon after treatment do most drug users relapse?"

Longitudinal Studies
The obvious way to study this question is to find a group of drug users who have undergone treatment, and study the same group of subjects over a particular period of time; this would be a longitudinal study. We could interview each subject every month, note whether they have resumed drug use or not, and count how many have resumed each month. Using the same subjects throughout keeps subject variables constant. However, it may be that a realistic period for such a study would be three years, whereas you wish to have the study completed within three months - a longitudinal study would not be appropriate.

Cross-Sectional Studies
A cross-sectional study would also interview former drug users at monthly intervals after receiving treatment, but rather than using the same subjects throughout, different groups of subjects would be used. (One group who had finished their treatment one month ago, another group who had finished their treatment two months ago, etc. Whilst this would take considerably less time, we have

no way of knowing whether each group is comparable with each other group. Also, circumstances may have changed as the different cohorts are studied. (Each representative group is called a cohort.) We can see how social attitudes may change over time and will have various effects on cohorts of different ages and may interfere with any conclusions we could draw in a cross-sectional study. We would be looking at attitudes formed 50-60 years ago possibly being acted out today.

Design issues
In terms of experimental design, a longitudinal study can be looked at as a repeated measures design, whereas a cross-sectional study would be independent groups. We would need to use this information when writing up our investigation or considering statistical analysis of our data. One feature of the example used is that we might expect our results to show a trend, i.e. in this case a consistent difference over time. For an example of how to display your data from these kinds of studies, turn to the example on page 40.

Correlation

So far we have looked at the experimental method where the independent variable is manipulated and the dependent variable is measured whilst all other variables are controlled. Any change in the *measured* variable is attributed to the *manipulated* variable - a cause and effect relationship. However, sometimes it is not possible, practicable or desirable to conduct an investigation in this way. It may be difficult to deliberately manipulate a particular variable, or it may be impossible to control other variables that may affect the result. In a correlational investigation, the two variables under study are simply measured and we look to see if there is a relationship between them.

> *A correlation indicates the degree to which two naturally occurring variables are related.*

There are three basic types of relationship between two variables, one is not better or worse that the others they are just different:

Positive Correlation: One variable increases, as the other variable increases.

> *Example:* If we were to get a number of subjects and measure the height and weight of each subject we would probably find that the taller the subjects are, the heavier they are. As height increases, weight increases.

Negative Correlation: One variable increases, as the other decreases.

> *Example:* We could look the relationship between the volume of your stereo system and the happiness of your neighbours. As the volume of your stereo system increases, the happiness of your neighbours decreases.

No Correlation: No real pattern to the results.

> *Example:* If we measured the shoe size and intelligence (using an intelligence test) of a group of subjects, we would probably find that there was no noticeable pattern in the results. Knowing their intelligence would not give us the confidence to buy the right size slippers for their birthday.

More Examples: Let's look at the relationship between ice cream sales and deaths by drowning at seaside resorts. If you collect the data and calculate a correlation coefficient (see later in this chapter) you will find that there is a very strong positive correlation. As ice cream sales at the seaside increase, more people drown. (Or as more people drown, so ice cream sales increase.)

We cannot, however, say that one has caused the other - simply that they go together. Although we can never prove this, we can make a guess at a likely explanation. In common with many correlations a third, hidden variable may be identified that is related to both. One guess may be temperature, so as temperature increases, more people buy ice creams *and* more people go swimming (so more are likely to drown).

Should we find, for example, a positive correlation between income and self-esteem it would be an error to think that high income *causes* high self-esteem and low income *causes* low self-esteem. It could be that there is a third factor involved and related to both. Education, perhaps, i.e. the more education, the greater the income and the more education the greater the self-esteem. At this point you may be thinking of someone that you know who has little money and feels great about themselves. Remember that, as with other techniques in research, correlation depends upon sampling and we are interested in general trends rather than individual cases.

Scattergrams - showing a correlation as a graph.
Having measured some subjects' scores on two variables (usually referred to as variable x and variable y) we can get a visual impression of the correlation, the degree to which they are related by drawing a simple kind of graph called a **scattergram**.

Worked example: Assume we were interested in the relationship between counselling ability and creativity. Each subject has taken a 'counselling ability test' and a 'creativity test' so we have a score for counselling ability and creativity for each subject. We call the counselling ability score, variable x and the creativity score, variable y. We tabulate the results as follows:

Subject	Score on variable x	Score on variable y
1	100	46
2	122	37
3	113	48
4	145	29
5	98	72
6	122	38
7	133	32
8	140	19
9	122	36
10	106	60

Next draw two axes on your graph paper covering the range of scores for each variable, with variable x along the horizontal axis and variable y on the vertical axis as illustrated in Chart 6.2.

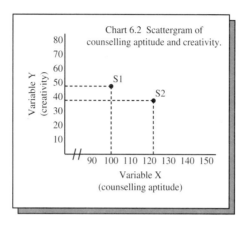

Then enter the scores by taking subject number 1's variable x score (100) and variable y score (46) and plotting them as illustrated in Chart 6.2 using dots or litte x's to mark the spot. Repeat this procedure for all ten subjects and you should end up with a graph that looks like Chart 6.3.

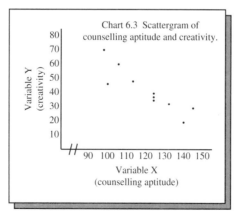

Now we can see a pattern to these results. Subjects who scored low on variable y scored high on variable x and vice versa (high on y and low on x). This pattern is typical of a negative correlation.

It's much easier to see a pattern in the results when drawn as a scattergram than it is if you gaze at columns of numbers. The following scattergrams illustrate typical correlations as indicated:

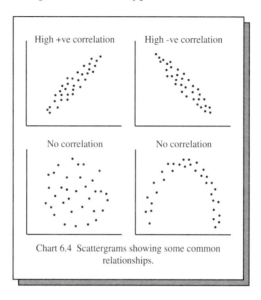

Chart 6.4 Scattergrams showing some common relationships.

If you look again at the last scattergram in the figure above you will notice something unusual. It demonstrates one of the limitations of correlations since there is clearly a relationship between variable x and variable y, described by the 'upside-down U' shaped scattergram. However because the slope to the left cancels out the slope to the right, the correlation for such a set of scores would be zero. This neatly illustrates why drawing scattergrams is always a good thing to do in addition to calculating a correlation coefficient.

Correlation Coefficients - defining the strength of the relationship

If a scattergram gives a visual impression of the relationship between two variables, then a correlation coefficient gives us an indication of both the strength and direction of a relationship as a numerical value.

Correlation coefficients range between -1 through 0 to +1. All the sign does is indicate the direction of the relationship (I explained this above in the scattergrams section). A correlation of 0 would indicate that there is no relationship between the two variables (as in the shoe size and intelligence example). The closer to 1 (or -1) the coefficient gets, the stronger the relationship between the variables until (and this is *very* rare in social science data) at 1 (or -1) we have a perfect relationship.

A correlation coefficient of .85 indicates a strong positive correlation.
A correlation coefficient of -.74 indicates a strong negative correlation.
A correlation coefficient of -.22 indicates a weak negative correlation.
A correlation coefficient of .16 indicates a weak positive correlation.

You may come across correlation coefficients when reading research papers or you may want to calculate one for your data. If you have collected data and wish to calculate a correlation coefficient, I have written a step-by-step procedure for calculating one of the most simple in Appendix III.

Hypotheses and Correlation
In a correlation we are looking for a *relationship* between two naturally-occurring variables and your hypotheses should reflect this. Other than this, the 'rules' for stating hypotheses are the same as for experiments.

Null hypothesis:"There will be no relationship between counselling ability and creativity."
Alternate hypothesis:"There will be a relationship between counselling ability and creativity." (Two-tailed.)
Or:"There will be a positive correlation between counselling ability and creativity." (One-tailed.)

In the case of correlation, a two-tailed hypothesis states that there will simply be a relationship, without predicting the direction whereas a one-tailed hypothesis states that not only will there be a relationship, but also whether it is expected to be positive or negative.

Significance and correlation

A significant correlation is one that is large enough that we are confident it is not due to chance, but due to a real replicable relationship. In other words if we were to take another similar sample of subjects, we would get a similar correlation.

In the case of correlation, sample size and significance are related in the sense that if you have a small sample (e.g. 10), you will need a very high correlation coefficient to achieve significance (around .60). Conversely if you have a large sample size (above 50 for example) you will need a relatively small correlation coefficient (around .25). A complicating factor is that the larger the sample size, the more difficult it is to get a large correlation coefficient.

A correlation coefficient is worth working out even if you have no intention of carrying your work through to the 'statistical significance' stage, since it, like measures of central tendency and dispersion, is telling you something about your data. You can always use a rough rule of thumb to tell you whether your correlation may be due to chance by using the numbers in the paragraph above.

Observational Methods

Observations are intended for accurate *description* and then hopefully meaningful *explanations* of behaviour. This method is primarily intended for the study of behaviour in natural settings where an experiment would not be possible or desirable because of the effect it may have on natural behaviour. Whilst the behaviour being observed should be natural and unmanipulated, the simple fact of being observed may itself have an effect on the behaviour of the subjects. As counsellors we know the disturbing effects of having our work observed! There are a number of ways of minimising this and other undesirable effects.

1. The subjects are simply allowed to become *accustomed to the presence* of the observers (or their apparatus). This does take time and if you wish to observe behaviour in a specific situation, such as a first counselling interview, then this may not be appropriate.

2. The observers (or their apparatus) could be *concealed* from the subjects. This would minimise the effects of being observed, but would create other problems. Visibility and lines of sight would become a problem, thus restricting the range of behaviour that could be observed, and there is also the ethical consideration of whether the subjects know that they are being observed.

3. This option is where the observer becomes part of the group that is being observed - *participant observation.* In some ways the study will become more realistic, but the behaviour of the observer may affect that of the other members of the group. They may also become involved in the process that is occurring, become less accurate or objective in their description of what is happening, and it is difficult for other observers to verify the observations made by the participant. It would be an extremely difficult study to replicate.

Observations are very good for showing sequences of events, and therefore could be thought to be good for showing how one behaviour causes another. But, it should be remembered that there will be a large number of uncontrolled variables in a natural situation, and this will make it difficult to infer 'cause and effect' relationships. It is also worth remembering that observations of this sort require constant description of behaviour. Even if some sort of shorthand code is developed for noting behaviours, an observation will generate a great deal of information, which will have to be presented in some way - if sequences of behaviour are to be shown, it is very difficult (if not impossible) to put this information in mathematical form.

So far we have assumed that the observation taking place is both natural and continuous. It may be that, in order to limit the amount of information generated or to restrict the range of behaviours studied, by imposing a degree of control over the environment, restricting the range of behaviour studied to pre-determined categories, or sampling behaviour at certain time intervals, rather than monitoring it continuously. Of course there will be advantages and disadvantages to each method.

Controlled or Structured Observation
If you wished to observe behaviour during counselling interviews, it may be the case that continuous, natural observation would be an appropriate method. However, if you wanted to observe a group session, the difficulties involved may cause you to consider imposing a degree of structure.

You may wish to control the environment to a degree by holding the session in a particular room because it offers good visibility. This imposition of a particular environment may have some effect on the behaviour of the subjects. It may also be the case that continuous monitoring and a full description of all behaviours is not possible. This requires incredibly fast recording or, if the recording is mechanical a huge amount of transcription. In any event you may have to structure your observation using one of the following methods:

1. Event Sampling
In this method the researcher has to produce a set of categories of behaviour, so to continue the group session example from above, a list of observable behaviours could be:

> Agrees, Disagrees, Gives Information, Seeks Information, Shows Aggression Shows Support, Shows Humour, Mediates.

Each time one of the behaviours occurs, a tick is placed against that category for either the whole group or individual group members. There are however, a number of problems with such a simple method:

Problem 1:

>It will, for example, show you the number of occurrences but not the sequence of behaviours. It could be that many people said 'I agree' after contributions at the beginning of a group, but that the whole second half of the group was taken up with a bitter disagreement. Just counting occurrences would miss this.

Problem 2:

>The categories themselves can be a problem. How well defined are they? The categories should be mutually exclusive, i.e. behaviours should only fit into one category with no overlap. In the above example would you know how to distinguish between 'Agrees' and 'Shows Support'.

Problem 3:

>If there is only one observer then objectivity becomes an issue of validity. (E.g. the humour category could be, to say the least, a matter of personal taste.) If there is more than one observer then inter-observer reliability (see page 32) becomes an issue.

Observation should not be seen as an easy option compared to experimentation. Observations require just as much planning, preparation and rigour as any other research method.

2. Time Sampling

Rather than continuously monitoring the behaviour of subjects, this method samples the behaviour of subjects at pre-determined time intervals, e.g. the behaviour of a particular subject may be noted every minute, or every ten minutes or whatever. Observations would continue at the given intervals until the observation period had ended. You could simply write down the behaviour to record it or use a category (see above). Whilst the main advantage of this method is to reduce the amount of information that has to be recorded, it both suffers from the same problems as event sampling and has one of its own:

Problem:

> You may fall prey to cycles of behaviour in a session which will distort your results. One way round this is to sample behaviour at random time intervals (use a random number table - see Appendix IV) although this is much more effort it could be worth it.

Content Analysis

It is possible to view many areas of human endeavour (e.g. media output) as human behaviour, and when this is sampled using the above methods, the content can be recorded and analysed. So we might conduct a content analysis of a news bulletin on the radio by taking a transcript and analysing its content. Or we may sample a whole day's television programmes every hour on the half hour. Content analysis is also an increasingly popular *narrative* technique when used on people's descriptions of their experiences. The same cautions regarding sampling of behaviour and observer validity and reliability apply.

Surveys and Questionnaires

Most surveys use some form of questionnaire, a fixed set of questions followed in a set pattern for all subjects. Three issues arise when we consider conducting a survey, firstly, sampling, secondly the design of the questionnaire and thirdly administering the questionnaire.

Sampling

Advanced researchers would talk about sampling stimuli (questions), sampling responses (answers) and sampling respondents (subjects), but at this level we need only attend to the problem of sampling subjects (obtaining the people who are going to answer our questions). We will be looking in a slightly less sophisticated way at questionnaire design in the next section.

We have covered most of the sampling issues in Chapter 4 called 'Distributions - Populations and Samples'. The main difference between a survey and other methods is the size of the sample.

Because there is no control of extraneous variables, and the measurements themselves are (peoples' opinions) are subject to unpredictable variation, the larger the survey sample the better. I can say this now in the certain knowledge that expense, time and effort will impose their own limits on your surveying endeavours. You will, no doubt, wish to use your survey or questionnaire results to generalise from your sample to the population in general and this will be the driving force behind your intentions. If your sample is not representative, you will not be able to generalise your findings with confidence and your efforts will have been in vain. A sample of around 10% of such a population would be very respectable.

The remaining question is what sort of sample should you go for. To answer this question I refer you to Chapter 4. There are advantages and disadvantages to each sampling method. For a simple study with a discrete population such as all the students at a particular College, the some form of stratified sampling is best.

Questionnaire Design
It may seem the easiest thing in the world to produce a set of questions and give them to subjects, but questionnaire design is an art in itself and there are several pitfalls awaiting the inexperienced.

Hint: Try to limit the number of items (questions). Besides overloading or boring your subjects (this will affect their responses), the sheer length of your questionnaire may well be the deciding factor as to whether the subject completes your questionnaire. Use only questions that are essential to your investigation.

Hint: Pilot your questionnaire at various stages of completion. This means try it out on a few subjects to see if it works, if there are too many items, missing items, offensive items, confusing items, ambiguous items, in appropriate instructions, etc. Piloting is essential.

Hint: You should also use a small group of subjects to make suggestions regarding what questions you should ask. This way you will be asking relevant questions rather than ones that you think are important. This helps you avoid the possibility of just finding what you wanted to find.

Hint: Think very carefully about the type of questions you ask. Try to avoid open questions, since you will only have the difficult job of categorising them later. Ask questions with YES-NO answers or on a scale from 1 (Very Satisfied) to 5 (Very Unsatisfied). This will also help you express your results numerically. There is a phenomenon called *regression to the mean* that not only afflicts statistics but also people. It means that people are likely to go for a middle of the road answer or a 'don't know' option if at all possible. So don't give them the opportunity of opting for a mid point by using a scale without one, i.e. with an even number of options; 1 - 6 for example.

Hint: You should consider how you ask the questions. You should not ask leading questions in a leading way, i.e. indicate the questioner's preference, e.g. "Would you agree that abortion is the senseless murder of innocent humans by selfish, self-centred women who will burn in hell for the rest of eternity? Yes or No?" You could re-word this so as to give no hint about your opinions, e.g. "Are you in favour of abortion on demand? Yes or No?"

Questionnaire Administration

Firstly, you will need to give some thought to maximising the response rate to your questionnaire. In other words, even though you select, say 100 subjects, only 60 of them may complete the questionnaire.

The best response rate is achieved by administering your questionnaire in person. In this case there will be little problem other than getting your selected subjects to agree to answer your questions. Even then, be prepared to have a number of refusals. It only gets worse from now on, since every other method gives you a much worse response rate. Here are some simple procedures to help maximise your response rate:

Hint: If you send the questionnaire out by post always include a covering letter explaining the purpose of the study.

Hint: You may offer anonymity to your respondents. Make sure you keep your promise and show that you have done if anyone checks.

Hint: Provide stamped addressed envelopes for subjects to send back completed questionnaires.

Hint: Aim for a 70-80% response rate. Below 50% and your sample runs the risk of becoming unrepresentative.

Hint: Always thank your respondents for taking part - in advance if at all possible.

Interviews

Administering your questionnaire in person is one of two types of interview you may wish to conduct as part of your data collection. You can choose an informal, unstructured interview or a formal, structured one. If you have prepared a set of questions in the form of a questionnaire, you will be conducting a formal, structured interview in which all subjects are submitted to the same procedure. The results are then more readily generalised. However, subjects are more likely to recognise the procedure as routine and clinical and be less spontaneous in their responses.

Since your intention will usually be to generalise your results, an informal interview is probably not the best method to use as the lack of standard procedures makes it difficult to control any stray variables and thus compare results from different subjects. The information gained is difficult to submit to any type of formal analysis, but it may be useful in formulating further questions for study. Also, there is a growing trend to use narrative evidence and submit it to content analysis. An unstructured interview is a suitable method to collect such data. The one remaining problem with this method is the tedium of transcription of the interview. A half hour interview can take several hours to transcribe and also contain a lot of irrelevant information.

Test yourself on Chapter 6 with these questions:

1. What features of the experimental method distinguish it from other methods?

2. List the advantages and disadvantages of repeated measures, matched pairs and independent groups designs

3. What would a correlation be used for?

4. How would you control for experimenter effects, demand characteristics and order effects?

5. What is the difference between longitudinal and cross-sectional studies?

Discussion Point

Only experimental methods can reveal cause and effect relationships, but the level of control is sometimes so intrusive that some people argue that the point of the experiment is lost. This could be particularly true when it comes to counselling studies, when the subjects might be at their most vulnerable. Do you think experiments are worth the bother? Do you think there is a better way of investigating counselling?

7 Reporting Your Work

Scientific Reports and Research Papers

Although you may have found the subject of your investigation very interesting indeed, it is unlikely that there would be a point to carrying out your research if you were not to communicate your findings to other people. Any study should culminate in a report that allows the reader to find out exactly what you did, why you did it, how it was done, what you found and why you found it.

What you have carried out is a scientific investigation, and it should be reported as such. To help you with this there are certain conventions regarding the manner in which it should be reported. There is a format to be followed which will be covered later, but there is also the matter of writing style.

Instructions on how to report studies usually indicate that they should be written in the 'third person passive'. Assuming that most readers are not English graduates, I will attempt to explain. The report should not contain words such as 'I', 'we' or 'you', in describing how the report was carried out. The study has been conducted by an experimenter on subjects, rather than by you on Pete, Jane, Chris, Tim and Ged. Do not include sentences such as "I decided to carry out an investigation...", this should become, "It was decided to investigate..." Similarly, "We told the subjects...", would become, "The subjects were told..." This convention should be observed throughout the report. When reporting your results, "I found that...", should be, "It was found that...", and when discussing the findings, "I think that...", can be replaced with, "The results suggest..." This may take a little bit of getting used to, but it will be worth it in the end as your report will take on the appearance of an objective and scientific paper.

At some point in your report, you will probably find that you need to include tables, diagrams and graphs. Besides the obvious need to give these a title, you should also give each one a reference, such as Table 1 or Figure 7. You can then refer back to these at other points in the written text (e.g. see Fig 7).

One final point before attempting to explain the contents of a report, you should keep detailed notes of procedures and methods used as you go along. This will be of considerable help when you come to write the report. From bitter experience, it is much easier to give details of how the investigation was conducted if you write up the details as soon as possible after the event.

The anatomy of a research paper
Your write-up should contain the following sections. Although you may not want to use these headings, you should organise your report so that information is easily found:

> *Title*
> *Abstract* (or Summary)
> *Introduction*
> *Method* - containing:
> > Subjects
> > Apparatus
> > Procedure
> > Design
> *Results*
> *Discussion*
> *References*
> *Appendices.*

Title
Quite simply, the title should explain clearly, in as few words as possible what the investigation is about. There are a few stock phrases to start your title, such as 'An Investigation into....' or 'A Study of....'

Examples: 'A Study of the Effects of Gestalt Therapy on the Perception of Domestic Furniture'. 'An Investigation into the Relationship Between Person-Centred Therapy and Increase in Personal Effectiveness.'

Abstract (or Summary)

Although this will be found right at the start of the finished report, it will actually be the last part that you write. It should provide a clear, and above all, concise summary of the report. Without using lengthy descriptions, it should explain what the study investigated, how this was done and what was found. No matter how complicated your research, the abstract should run to no more than 200 words.

There are logical reasons for producing an abstract, and once you start reading in preparation for your own research you will be very glad of them. There are literally thousands of research papers written every year, possibly a large proportion in the area in which you are interested. No one has time to read all of them to find out what they are about and whether they are relevant, so the abstracts come in very handy. Collections of abstracts are available in your local college library.

Introduction

If you could visualise the introduction as a shape, then it would be an inverted triangle, starting out wide at the top and narrowing as it approaches the end. Your introduction will start out providing a general description of the area under investigation and become more specific as the focus narrows to your particular study.

Example: If your study is concerned with the self image you would start the introduction with a definition of the concept and some comment on its relationship to behaviour. This could then be narrowed to a more specific consideration of the factors that affect the self concept, such as the reactions of other people to behaviour. In this part of your introduction you should be making reference to the studies and findings of other researchers in this particular area of investigation.

At the end of your introduction you should clearly state your hypotheses, anyone reading the report will know exactly where to look for these and will know precisely what the study is intending to investigate.

Note: Throughout your introduction you will be making reference to work carried out by other people that is relevant to your investigation. This should always be acknowledged by giving the name of the author or researcher and the date of publication in brackets immediately after the reference. For example, if you have referred to work published by Coopersmith in 1967, the inserting (Coopersmith 1967) will acknowledge the source. Full details of the work you have quoted or described should be given in the Reference section at the end of the report (see later for details).

Method

This section is concerned with the mechanics of conducting your study. Remember that one of the criteria of a good study is that other people should be able to replicate it. The Method section should give sufficient precise detail that anyone reading it should be able to reproduce your study. To make this section easier, it is broken down into four sub-sections, each dealing with a specific aspect of the mechanics of the study.

1) Subjects: Generally, this will be a relatively short section, giving brief details of the subjects who took part in the study - sufficient that a similar group could be assembled again. Details to be given should include, number of subjects used, their age range, their sex and details of the population from which they were drawn. For example, 25 subjects were used, aged between 20 and 42. Twenty-one of them were female and 4 male. All the subjects were nurses.

If there are any important and relevant pieces of information about the subjects chosen, then these should also be given. For example "All subjects had attempted suicide within the past 12 months."

2) Apparatus: This section should give details of all equipment or materials used in the investigation. In most cases a list of these will suffice, though examples of materials should be included in the appendix section, and reference should be made to this. For example, if you have used a questionnaire this should be listed, and an example placed in the appendix. The appendix is also the place for details of any piece of apparatus you may have constructed yourself.

Where you have used a specific piece of apparatus, details of the make and model should be given. There's no need to be too specific with this; a pencil is a pencil! If you think it necessary, a diagram should be included giving details of how equipment was set up or positioned.

3) Procedure: Exactly how the study was conducted should be dealt with in this section. Again, sufficient details should be given to allow anyone to repeat the procedure. It is a good idea to set out step by step what the experimenter did as well as details of what the subjects were required to do. If instructions were issued to subjects, these should be reported, though you may prefer to state that the standardised instructions were issued to subjects and then include a copy of these in the appendix.

Other details necessary for replication should also be included, such as time allowed per subject, how many trials subjects were allowed, what order the procedure followed, etc. In fact anything and everything that was part of the procedure of the experiment but be careful about including truly irrelevant detail. Remember, you are writing about things that have already happened, so the procedure should be written in the past tense. Also do not use the 'I' and 'we' words.

4) Design: This section deals with the scientific aspects of the study. How (or if) *variables* were manipulated or measured or controlled. It should start with the details of the actual method used, and what variables were involved. For example, if you have conducted an experiment, details should be given of which experimental design was used, and then identify the different conditions of the experiment. Also, the independent and dependent variables should be identified. The section should then give details of how all other unwanted variables were controlled. For example, that fact that all the trials were conducted in the same room, controlled environmental factors (variables) such as heating, lighting and background noise, or the fact that *counterbalancing* was used to control *order effects*. Again, if standardised instructions have been used this should be mentioned as this controls for the possibility of the experimenter treating subjects differently (experimenter effect). Basically, details of anything that was done to avoid unwanted variables interfering with the study should be included.

This should be done whatever the method used; if a correlation had been conducted, then details of the variables under investigation should be given. Also, details should be included as to how subjects were selected; if they were a random sample, how this was achieved, etc. Again, as much relevant detail as possible should find its place here.

Results
The results' section of your report should be as brief and concise as possible. Unless they are absolutely necessary, this is not the place to put in large tables of data (they go in the appendix), it's the place for figures that give a *summary* of the results, means, totals, modes, ranges, etc.

The first step in this section should be to explain what has been done to the results obtained. For example, "The means of the experimental conditions were calculated", or "The number of Yes and No answers were counted", or "A correlation coefficient was calculated". After this, the results should be clearly presented, e.g. a table with histogram or scattergram. If hypotheses have been stated, you can then indicate which hypothesis appears to have been supported - state the hypothesis at this point. A brief description of the results can also be given whether one condition appears to have produced better results than the other, or whether there is a strong correlation, or a general degree of satisfaction. Finally, if you do wish to illustrate further you results with graphs, keep them as simple and effective as possible.

Note: Examples of calculations performed should not be included in the results' section, but once again consigned to an appendix, where anyone who desperately needs stimulation in their life can pore over your data, and check your calculations.

Discussion
The main aim of this section is to assess the degree to which your results satisfy the original aims of the study and to offer an interpretation of your results. A very quick description of a discussion section would be to say that it covered:
  1) What the results show.
  2) How this fits with previous work in the area.
  3) What caused the results.
  4) Where do we go from here?

1) What the results show: The first stage in your discussion section should be a description of your results and highlight the basic trends that have emerged. This should not be a simple case of re-describing the data, but one of pointing to interesting areas from the results.

2) How this fits with previous work in the area: After this there should be some consideration as to how your results compare with previous research and theory. Are you results consistent with those of previous studies? You will of course have made reference to the most relevant previous studies in your introduction, and attention should be drawn to these.

3) What caused your results: Having completed the above, you should then offer an explanation as to what caused the results. You can do this in either one, or preferably both, of two ways.

Firstly, you can offer an interpretation of the results in theoretical terms;identifying the processes that have contributed to your results. Here you may make reference to other theories, or offer your own explanation of the results - a combination of the two may be appropriate. The other type of explanation for the results is possible shortcomings with the method you have used in your study. These methodological errors should be identified, with the comment as to how they could have affected the results. It is important that any criticism should be constructive, and besides identifying the problems, solutions as to how these could be remedied, if the study were to be repeated, should be included.

4) Where do we go from here? Finally, comment should be made on the applicability of the results. Having gained a body of knowledge or findings, how is this going to be used in practice. Is it going to lead to better procedures, has it given us a better understanding of a process? Also, what does the study lead on to? Do you have any suggestions as to the next stage in the research following on from the present study?

References
It is important to give details of all source material, be it journal articles, books or chapters in books. There is a standard procedure for giving references. They should be arranged in alphabetical order according to the names of the authors. The details of each should be arranged in the following sequence:

1) Name of the author(s).
2) The date of publication.
3) Title of the book or article. In the case of books, it is customary to place the title in *italics*. In the case of journal articles, these are usually placed in quotation marks.
4) If the reference is a book, give the name and place of the publisher of the book. If the reference is an article in a journal, then give the name of the journal (in *italics*).
5) In the case of journal articles, you should give the volume number and the page numbers.

Note : If the research you have used is a chapter written by one person, but reproduced in a book edited by another the procedure is slightly different. The first three steps are the same as above, giving the author, date and name of the chapter or article. This should then be followed by "in...", followed by the name of the book (in italics of course), the name of the editor followed by the word "ed." At this point the location and name of the publishers should be given.

The following are examples of each;
>a) a book: Allport, G. (1956) *The Nature of Prejudice.* Reading, Mass., Addison-Wesley.
>b) a journal article: Asch,S.E. (1946) 'Forming impressions of personality', *Journal of Abnormal and Social Psychology*, 41, 258-90
>c) a chapter in a book: Backman, C.W., and Secord, P.F. (1966) 'The Compromise Process and the Affect Structure of Groups'. In *Problems in Social Psychology: Selected Readings.* C.W. Backman and P.F. Secord, eds., New York, McGraw-Hill.

and of course
>Liptrot, D. and Sanders, P. *An Incomplete Guide to Inferential Statistics for Counsellors.* Manchester, PCCS. (In press)

Appendices
This is the catch-all section at the end of the report which contains anything that is relevant, but has not yet been included elsewhere. Things like tables of raw data, calculations, examples of materials, standardised instructions, etc. Each different type of item should be placed in a separate appendix, which should then be labelled so that reference may be made to it in the text (e.g. see Appendix 3).

Writing Annual and 'Business' Reports

There may be occasions when you may have been asked to collect information and comment on your findings in a less stylised manner, either as an end of year summary or as a specific investigation into some aspect of the organisation.

Note: Before you begin your report make sure you know exactly
• what is required of you if you are writing it for another person or,
• what you are hoping it to achieve if you have generated the report yourself.

As with scientific reports these 'annual' reports have a specific format to help both with their writing and with their reading. This format, to some extent, varies according to the purpose of the report, but as a rule they include the following headings:

> *1) Introduction*
> *2) Method of investigation*
> *3) Findings*
> *4) Conclusions*
> *5) Recommendations*

These headings can be extended to show their contents:

> *1) Which organisation, and who in that organisation, is the report for?*
> *The area(s) covered by the investigation.*
> *What is the purpose of the report?*
> *2) The method(s) of obtaining the relevant information.*
> *3) The findings that emerged from the investigation.*
> *4) A summary of the main points of the findings.*
> *5) The actions recommended for the future.*

Some reports do not require division into these five headings, but even if they are not all needed, keeping them in mind will ensure that important areas are not omitted. If your report is likely to be longer then 400 words then include these five headings to make the report more accessible to the reader. Let your personal judgement and the requirements of the organisation be your guide. Remember, always to think of your target reader and gear your writing style, and the organisation of your points, to them. Your report may benefit if you avoid jargon where possible and aim for simplicity and brevity.

1) Introduction
Rather than making reference to, or comparisons with, previous studies, as in theoretical reports, it would be more appropriate to start with a brief description of the organisation and its aims. From there, you can refer to previous reports and performance of the organisation, etc. This will form a basis for comparison and comment in the Conclusions and Recommendations sections of your report.

You can also note who, within the organisation, the report is for, why they commissioned it and what areas or issues are to be studied. Remember that the purpose of this section is to set the scene and to inform the reader of the background to your report. If any others were involved in carrying out the investigation we you need to mention them here.

Example: You are doing an investigation into the success, or otherwise, of a charity telephone help line offering help to pregnant couples. You have been asked by the agency manager to find out the numbers and types of callers this year, to compare them to those in previous years and to other similar organisations.

2) Method of Investigation
Here you will need to lay out briefly, but clearly, the methods you used to gather the required information.

Example: You will indicate how you went about collecting the information and what sort of information you were interested in. For instance, the numbers of callers, perhaps over the four different yearly quarters, how you placed the different types of caller into separate categories (age, sex, other children, stage of pregnancy, etc.), how often the same callers used your service, average length of call, etc.

3) Findings

This section will contain the information collected. How you convey this information will depend on the amount collected, the type collected and the clearest method available to you (graphs, pie charts, tables, etc.) You may need to divide the information into numbered headings that can be referred to later if necessary.

4) Conclusions

This should be a brief, though not therefore, unimportant part of the report. The conclusions to your findings may seem obvious, but they need stating nevertheless for those who may not be as familiar with the subject as you are.

Example: You may have found that your telephone agency is used mainly by the 16 - 25 age group, most of whom are women and a large proportion of these being single. Where men use the service their calls are generally much shorter than those made by women.

5) Recommendations

Note: Do not make recommendations unless you have been asked to do so; they may be unwelcome or seen as presumptuous.

This is often the most challenging (and enjoyable) section; both for the reader and the writer. There may be a temptation to make recommendations that reflect your own personal views; try, at all costs, to resist this temptation. The challenge comes from teasing out the recommendations that are 'hidden' in the findings. Multiple recommendations are best numbered and linked to the numbered findings.

Example: From the findings it may be clear that you need to recommend that the agency should advertise more specifically to make the service more accessible to men, and to employ more male counsellors. You may feel that you need to recommend in-service training for counsellors so that the agency can offer face-to-face counselling for those who call regularly, or for others who prefer a less 'anonymous' form of help.

Finally

The completed report should be dated and signed. If the report has been produced by a number of people their names are usually included in the introduction and the report signed by the group leader (if there was one).

Before you hand it over it's always worth spending time to check the report through for errors of spelling, grammar or maths; if possible get another person not closely involved in it to check it through too. This extra effort saves the embarrassing sinking feeling and loss of Street Cred when you look at your copy, just after the report has left your hands, to find that you'd spelt your boss's name wrongly.

Sums - A Quick Refresher

Basic Arithmetic

Addition

If the numbers to be added are all of the same sign, add in the usual way:

$$
\begin{array}{cc}
+12 & -12 \\
+\ +5 & +\ -5 \\
\hline
=+17 & =-17
\end{array}
$$

When there are a mixture of +ve and -ve signs, a good procedure is to add up the signs separately then combine the two:

$$
\begin{array}{l}
-10 \\
-11 \\
+20 \\
+13 \\
-16 \\
+12
\end{array}
\qquad
\begin{array}{l}
\text{Adding the +ve numbers gives } +45 \\
\text{Adding the -ve numbers gives } \underline{\ -37} \\
\hphantom{\text{Adding the -ve numbers gives }} = +8
\end{array}
$$

Subtraction

Again this should be straight forward when both numbers are positive. If you have a negative number in your sum, the simple rule is:

Change the sign of the number you are taking away and add.

$$
\begin{array}{llllll}
67 & \text{becomes} & 67 & -23 & \text{becomes} & -23 \\
-\ -51 & & +\ 51 & -\ -8 & & +\ 8 \\
\hline
+118 & & +118 & -15 & & -15
\end{array}
$$

Multiplication
The simple rule is:
> *Like signs multiplied together give a positive product, different signs multiplied together give a negative product.*

So:

+ve times +ve = +ve

-ve times -ve = +ve

+ve times -ve = -ve

-ve times +ve = -ve

Division
Much the same as multiplication, the rule says:
> *When dividing two like signed numbers, the quotient is positive, when dividing differently signed numbers, the quotient is negative.*

So:

+ve divided by +ve = +ve

-ve divided by -ve = +ve

+ve divided by -ve = -ve

-ve divided by +ve = -ve

Zero
Multiplying any number by zero, gives a product of zero.

$$1 \times 0 = 0 \qquad 10,000 \times 0 = 0 \qquad 237.987 \times 0 = 0$$

Decimals
When using decimals, there is generally no need to have strings of numbers after the decimal point. The number of decimal places you should work to is dependent upon the thing you are measuring and the range of values, e.g. when measuring your dependent variable in whole numbers and over a small range of values, it is reasonable to take a mean value to two decimal places. When using a large range of measurements, e.g. 0 - 100, it is sensible to take a mean value to only one decimal place.

When multiplying decimals the number of decimal places in the product is equal to the sum of the number of decimal places in the numbers being multiplied:

$$7.04 \times 5.2 = 36.080 \qquad\qquad 9.01 \times 3.2 = 28.832$$

When dividing decimals, the number of decimal places in the quotient is equal to the number of decimal places in the dividend (the number being divided) minus the number of decimal places in the denominator (the number the dividend is divided by):

$$.00016/0.2 = 0.0008$$

Brackets
Brackets in an arithmetic expression mean that:

1. There is a calculation to be done inside the brackets:
$$(2+3) = 5$$

2. You should do the calculations inside the brackets first.

3. You must multiply the results of the calculations inside the brackets by the numbers immediately in front of the brackets on the outside:
$$6(2+3) = 6\,(5) = 6 \times 5 = 30$$

4. Or you must multiply the results of the calculations inside the with the results of any other 'inside brackets' calculations:
$$(1+5)(2+3) = (6)\,(5) = 6 \times 5 \quad 30$$

5. If there are brackets inside brackets, you should work from the inside out:
$$6[2(4+5)] = 6[2(9)] = 6[2 \times 9] = 6[18] = 6 \times 18 = 108$$

6. Obey any signs between brackets or between brackets and numbers outside:
$$(2+3) - (4+5) + (8-3) = (5) - (9) + (5) = 5 - 9 + 5 = 1$$

Formulae

There is a simple mnemonic 'BODMAS' that will help you remember the order in which to do things when calculating a formula:

B (Brackets)   Do what's inside the brackets first.

O (Over and Under)   If there is a fraction, complete the calculations over and under the line before working the fraction out:

$$\frac{2+3}{16-6} = \frac{5}{10} = \frac{1}{2} = 0.5$$

D (Divide)   Do divisions before other calculation.

M (Multiplication)   Do multiplications next.

A (Add)   Next do additions.

S (Subtraction)   Lastly do subtractions.

Ranking

This is a simple procedure in which the numbers in a set are arranged in order from the lowest to the highest or vice versa and assigned *ranks*. A rank is the position number (like records in the charts - at number one this week, etc.). So in order to rank the following numbers from highest to lowest, we firstly put them in order, then assign ranks as follows:

5, 3, 7, 12, 8, 9, 4, 14

Put in order from highest to lowest:

14, 12, 9, 8, 7, 5, 4, 3

Then assign ranks:

14	rank 1
12	rank 2
9	rank 3
8	rank 4
7	rank 5
5	rank 6
3	rank 7

There are no problems with it until you get what's known as tied ranks, i.e. two or more numbers occupying the same rank.

The solution is simple, the rank you allocate to any tied numbers is equal to *the mean of the ranks they would have occupied had they been different.* So to rank the following numbers from highest to lowest:

9, 3, 12, 9, 4, 7, 4, 2, 4, 6 (put in order as before):

12, 9, 9, 7, 6, 4, 4, 4, 3, 2 Then allocated ranks:

12	Start with rank 1 unless the first positions tie	rank 1
9	These two would have occupied ranks 2 and 3	rank 2.5
9	so the mean of 2 + 3 = (2 + 3)/2 = 2.5	rank 2.5
7	The next available rank after 2 and 3 is	rank 4
6		rank 5
4	These three would have occupied ranks	rank 7
4	6, 7, and 8 so the mean of 6 + 7 + 8 =	rank 7
4	(6 + 7 + 8)/3 = 7	rank 7
3	The next available rank after 6, 7, and 8 is	rank 9
2		rank 10

NOTE
Two good tips when ranking a set of numbers are
1. Do it in rough first. This applies to all maths and arithmetical calculations.

2. To write out the number of ranks to be awarded at the side or along the bottom of the page before you begin. (The number of ranks to be awarded is simply equal to the number of numbers in the series to be ranked.) So in the example above, we would write

1 2 3 4 5 6 7 8 9 10

As each rank is used or allocated it should be crossed out:

1 2 3 4 5 6 7 8 9 10

thus making sure that we don't miss any. (There's nothing worse than ranking 32 scores only to find that you've only used 31 when you get to the end!)

Ranking as a technique crops up in a number of statistical procedures that you may find useful if you are going to do some low-key research. These are called *non-parametric* statistics and are covered in other books to be found in our 'Further Information' section on page 160. One such non-parametric procedure is the Spearman's Rank-Order Correlation Coefficient on page 155. You should have no problems with the Spearman's Rho, as it's called, if you follow the guidelines above.

The "Rules" of Graphing - A Quick Summary

General Rules on Presentation.

• The graph or table is the focal point of any summarised information. The reader's eyes are drawn to it first, so make it simple and attractive.

• Don't try to make it too big or too complicated. A graph or table can contain too much data.

• If your reader is put off by or doesn't understand a cluttered or overcomplicated table or graph, you have failed.

• Don't use colour unless you have good quality computer-generated graphics facilities, it doesn't photocopy well and might end up looking like a primary school nature project.

• Give every table and graph a title and clear labels for the rows and columns if it's a table and both axes if it's a graph. Put your scale and units of measurement clearly on each axis where appropriate.

• Position your table or graph on the page so that it is clearly visible, has enough space around it and isn't cramped.

• If you're writing a report or thesis and you have many graphs and tables of results it is usual (though not always so) to put the bulk of them in an appendix at the end of your report before the references.

Tables

• Use tables when you have to summarise data which you will later represent in a graph.

• If your study is an experiment, the usual results summary table will be put together like this: (see overleaf)

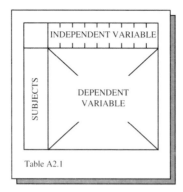

Table A2.1

• Tables can be used to help in some calculations by containing small parts of larger calculations such as the 'scores squared' bit of the standard deviation formula or correlation coefficient see pages 59 and 157.

• Don't be afraid of putting a fair amount of information in a table. What you mustn't sacrifice is its readability, i.e. if there are too many rows or columns too close together the eyes can get 'lost' in the middle of the table.

Graphs

The two lines that form the framework of a graph are called axes. The horizontal axis is called the *x-axis* or *abscissa*, the vertical axis is called the *y-axis* or *ordinate*.

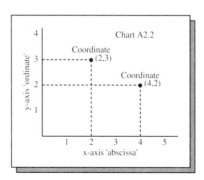

• When plotting a graph, look up the x-axis value fist, followed by the y-axis value. These are called the *co-ordinates*.

• Plot all your co-ordinates before joining them up to make i) a curve or frequency polygon or ii) a histogram (bar chart).

• Group bars together in series if you're trying to suggest that they go together:

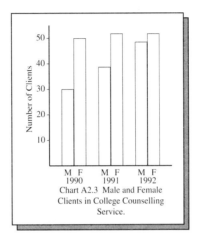

Chart A2.3 Male and Female Clients in College Counselling Service.

If you're drawing a curve or bar chart and you want to represent the overall shape of the distribution rather than detailed comparison between categories, choose x-axis intervals that are close together:

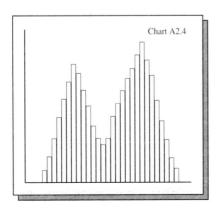

Chart A2.4

You can, if it helps display your data better, turn histograms on their side (the press use this sort of presentation quite frequently), or use symbols and graphics instead of bars:

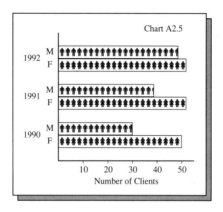

Pie Charts
These are best used to portray parts of a whole, proportions or percentages.

If you don't have a protractor to draw the pie chart, use the following 'All Purpose Pie Chart' by working the proportions out as percentages (rather than degrees) then tracing the segments from the diagram. All combinations are possible by just putting together the appropriate segments below. Feel free to photocopy this chart to facilitate tracing.

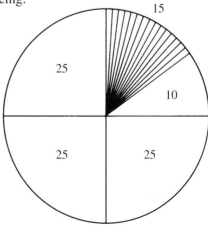

How to Calculate a Correlation Coefficient

There is a variety of procedures for calculating a correlation coefficient. The one that has been chosen here is the Spearman's Rank Order Correlation Coefficient. (For the sake of ease I will abbreviate correlation coefficient to CC for the rest of this appendix.)

Before I go any further, and on a note of self-disclosure, I would like to dedicate this section to my Maths teacher, who promised to give up teaching if I ever passed my Maths 'O' level. If I can do it, so can you (though preferably with the help of a calculator).

The Calculation
In order to calculate the CC you need to know how to rank a set of scores. If you need to refresh your ranking skills turn to Appendix I.

> *Example*
> Imagine we wanted to look at the relationship between counselling ability and creativity. We have got 10 subjects, and have given each of them a counselling ability and a creativity test. We will now look to see if there is a correlation between the two sets of scores.

Step 1
Construct a table like the one below. The number of rows in the table will obviously depend on the number of subjects you have, but the number of columns is always the same.

Into the second column, insert the scores on the first variable (in this case counselling ability) and in the third column, insert the scores on the second variable (creativity). It is usual to refer to these as variable x and variable y:

subject	score on variable x	score on variable y	rank of variable x	rank of variable y	difference	difference squared
1	100	46				
2	122	37				
3	113	48				
4	145	29				
5	93	72				
6	122	38				
7	133	32				
8	140	19				
9	122	36				
10	106	60				

Step 2
In the fourth column (headed 'rank of variable x') rank all the scores on the first variable from the lowest to the highest. Repeat this procedure for the other set of scores, placing the ranks in the 5th column (headed 'rank of variable y').

Step 3
Find the difference between the ranks for each individual subject. This is done by subtracting the ranks for variable y from the ranks of variable x; and enter this in the 6th column, which is headed Differences.

For example, subject one has a rank of 2 for the first variable and a rank of 7 from the second. So 2 - 7 = -5. If you do have a minus figure, keep the minus sign in the table for the time being, we shall be getting rid of it shortly.

Step 4
Now square each of the difference scores, and insert these in the last column.

subject	score on variable x	score on variable y	rank of variable x	rank of variable y	difference	difference squared
1	100	46	2	7	-5	25
2	122	37	6	5	1	1
3	113	48	4	8	-4	16
4	145	29	10	2	8	64
5	93	72	1	10	-9	81
6	122	38	6	6	0	0
7	133	32	8	3	5	25
8	140	19	9	1	8	64
9	122	36	6	4	2	4
10	106	60	3	9	-6	36

Step 5
Now add up all the scores in the last column.

In the above example, this gives us a total of 316.
If you want to know, what you have just worked out is Σd^2
Σ stands for the sum of (or total).
d^2 stands for the squared differences.

Step 6
Take the total you have just worked out and multiply it by 6.

In the example above this would give us 6 x 316 = 1896
We would refer to this as $6 \Sigma d^2$

Step 7
Count the number of subjects (call this N for short).

In the example N = 10.

Step 8
Square your N score, and then subtract 1.
> In the example N squared (N^2) is 10 x 10 = 100.
> And by subtracting 1 we get 99.
> The calculation above can be written as (N^2 - 1).

Step 9
Multiply the figure you have just obtained (N^2 - 1) by N.
This calculation would be N (N^2 - 1)
> So in the example, N^2 - 1 is 99
> and N is 10 so 10 x 99 = 990.

Step 10
Go back to the figure you got in Step 6 (which we called 6 Σd^2).
Divide this by the figure you obtained in Step 9 (which we called)
N (N^2 - 1)
> So in this case it would be $\dfrac{6 \Sigma d^2}{N (N^2 - 1)}$ or $\dfrac{1896}{990}$ = 1.91

> I expect you got a lot more figures on the calculator, but only
> use the first two after the decimal point.

Step 11 (The last lap)
Subtract the figure you got in the last stage from 1. This gives us
our Correlation Coefficient.
> In the example CC = 1 - 1.91 = - 0.91
> CC = - 0.91

The final figure (the CC) shows us that there is a high negative
correlation between counsellor ability and creativity. So what this
indicates is that, as counsellor ability increases, creativity decreases
(or vice versa).

If you have followed the calculation through from the start, what
you have calculated is the following formula:

$$\textbf{Correlation Coefficient} = 1 - \frac{6 \Sigma d^2}{N (N^2 - 1)}$$

Random Number Table

Rows	01	02	03	04	05	06	07	08	09	10	11	12	13	14	15	16	17	18	19	20
01	7	5	9	1	0	7	4	0	1	0	7	7	3	6	9	4	8	7	0	2
02	8	2	7	3	9	8	4	0	6	9	2	3	2	8	0	7	5	2	2	4
03	5	3	4	1	7	5	4	8	3	7	4	8	5	7	2	3	2	1	6	6
04	2	6	3	3	9	2	8	1	9	4	0	6	3	2	0	5	4	6	7	8
05	9	8	5	2	0	2	7	8	5	4	3	2	8	2	8	6	7	6	3	2
06	0	9	8	4	0	4	3	9	9	0	7	1	8	5	4	9	9	5	2	1
07	1	4	7	9	3	9	4	8	3	3	8	9	2	0	0	7	3	9	2	5
08	4	1	3	4	8	1	6	5	9	6	2	0	6	4	6	1	6	8	1	7
09	9	2	8	1	6	9	2	3	1	9	8	8	6	8	7	0	3	9	2	4
10	6	4	9	1	2	2	7	2	0	3	9	3	8	6	6	5	0	5	5	5
11	6	0	1	6	9	1	6	3	5	1	7	2	6	5	9	0	6	0	3	8
12	7	5	9	8	3	4	4	1	0	4	6	9	6	2	7	5	8	4	7	3
13	5	8	1	3	3	1	0	0	1	1	5	6	2	9	2	6	2	9	9	8
14	9	1	4	7	5	4	9	3	4	3	1	9	4	2	2	5	1	8	9	1
15	9	3	6	5	1	7	7	5	6	3	5	2	0	1	6	6	8	7	0	5
16	3	8	1	6	4	6	4	3	0	6	1	3	4	1	7	7	9	8	8	6
17	9	0	3	1	7	6	8	8	6	6	3	0	8	0	1	8	2	2	5	4
18	1	6	1	4	3	8	5	5	0	7	7	1	8	6	5	7	9	4	8	7
19	0	9	2	5	5	2	0	2	3	9	1	3	8	7	5	3	2	5	4	9
20	6	8	0	3	7	6	7	1	3	5	6	1	5	5	9	7	0	6	7	5

Use the table as follows: Suppose that 200 clients used the counselling service last year and we wish to select 20 at random to give them a questionnaire. Number the clients from 01 to 200. Pick an arbitrary starting point on the table (close your eyes and use a pin if you like). Then proceed in any direction taking numbers in threes. If you come across a number larger than 200, ignore it and continue. When you come to the edge of the table, change direction or find a new starting point. Eg start from row 17, column 2 and move right. Take 031, ignore 768, 866 and 308, taking 018, ignoring 225. I start again at row 6 column 20 and move left etc.

Further Information

Addresses

Advice, Guidance and Counselling Lead Body Secretariat, 40a High St, Welwyn, Herts, AL6 9EQ.

Association for the Teaching of Psychology (ATP) c/o The British Psychological Society, St Andrews House, 48 Princess Rd East, Leicester, LE 1 7DR.

British Association for Counselling, 1 Regent Place, Rugby, CV21 2PJ.

The British Psychological Society, St Andrews House, 48 Princess Rd East, Leicester, LE 1 7DR.

Further Reading

Books
Liptrot, D. and Sanders, P. *An Incomplete Guide to Inferential Statistics for Counsellors*, Manchester: PCCS (In press)
Miller, S. *Experimental Design and Statistics*, Routledge
Robson, C. *Experiment, Design and Statistics* in Psychology, Penguin

Journals
Occasional counselling-related research articles can be found in:
British Journal of Guidance and Counselling, published by Hobsons
Counselling, published by the British Association for Counselling
The Psychologist, published by The British Psychological Society

References

Rogers, Carl R. (1951) *Client Centred Therapy*, Boston: Houghton Mifflin.
Davies, G., Howarth, G., and Hirschler, S. (1992) *Ethics in Psychological Research*, Leicester: ATP Publications.

Glossary

Alternate hypothesis - This is the hypothesis that states that something will happen as a result of the investigation.

Analysis - Taking things or ideas apart, or separating things into their constituent parts to see how they fit together. (See also *reductionism*.)

Arithmetic mean - The total of all the scores divided by the number of scores; a measure of *central tendency*.

Asymmetrical distribution - A *distribution* of scores that do not cluster evenly about the mid point.

Bell-shaped curve - The shape of the curve indicating a *normal distribution*.

Bimodal - Having two *modes*.

Central tendency - The natural tendency of scores to cluster about the mid point.

Chi-squared - The statistical test that is applied to a particular form of independent groups design where the experimenter is looking for the degree of association between two variables.

Cluster sample - This is a *sample* in which a set number of subjects are chosen from a cluster or naturally occurring group, e.g. people in a family, or streets.

Concurrent validity - Where we compare our measure with another measure of the same thing taken at the same time.

Consistency - See *reliability*.

Construct - An idea that we create about how our world works and the 'things' that exist in it.

Construct validity - This is a form of validity that attempts to see how far the theoretical notion (*construct*) on which a measure is based is what it says it is.

Continuous measurement - Measurements that can be broken down into partial or fractional units, e.g. minutes and seconds.

Convenience and opportunity sample - A *sample* selected purely for convenience, when the opportunity arises.

Correlation - When two variables have a relationship though not necessarily a causal one.

Cross-sectional study - A study conducted at one point in time where subjects or events are sampled from each of successive cohorts.

Cumulative - Where the points plotted on a graph, or the figures used are running totals.

Data - Verifiable facts and measurements that we can collect about the world.

Demand characteristics - Where a person, e.g. the subject in an experiment, tries to work out what they should do in a given situation, i.e. to 'do what they're supposed to'.

Demographic - Statistics carrying information about human *populations*, e.g. age, sex, place of work, living conditions, etc.

Dependent variable - The *variable* that changes (measurably) as a result of the manipulation of the *independent variable*.

Descriptive statistics - Summarising and describing results in numbers.

Deviation - In the statistical sense this is how far a score is from a fixed point in a *distribution* such as the *mean*.

Discrete measurement - Measurements that can only be expressed in whole units or categories, e.g. male and female, age groups.

Dispersion - This is the degree to which the scores in a *distribution* are spread out.

Distribution - The pattern of occurrence of scores along a measurement scale.

Dualism - The idea that the mind and body are two separate entities.

Empirical - Relying on observation and measurement, not just theory or ideas.

Experimenter effect - An effect where the experimenter can themselves influence the results.

Extraneous variables - Unwanted variables that must be eliminated or kept constant by the researcher.

Face validity (also surface validity) - Where the validity of the measure is judged simply on whether it seems to be, or looks, appropriate.

Fatigue effect - An effect where a subject's performance tails off towards the end of a series of trials.

Frequency distribution - A graph showing the pattern of occurrence of frequencies of scores along a measurement scale.

Frequency data - This is where things are counted in categories.

Generalisation - The application of principles learned from a *sample* to the *population* from which the sample was drawn.

Holism - Another term for *synthesis* (see below), e.g. applied to human illness as holistic medicine.

Hypothesis - A statement of belief about the world, that is, as yet, unknown.

Hypothetico-deductive method - A scientific method whereby we formulate a *hypothesis* that predicts what is going to happen in a given situation then test it.

Independent groups - Two groups of different subjects who perform separately from each other in the different conditions of the experiment.

Independent variable - The *variable* that is manipulated by the researcher.

Inter-observer reliability - The degree to which two or more observers agree on what they've observed.

Interval scale of measurement - A method of measuring where the 'items' measured are ranked and where the gaps between the 'items' are equal, e.g. degrees of temperature.

IQ (Intelligence Quotient) - mental age divided by chronological age.

Longitudinal study - A type of study where subjects are tested at intervals over a period of time.

Matched pairs design - this involves matching the subjects into pairs on the basis of variables that you consider are relevant to the experiment.

Mean - See *arithmetic mean.*

Median - This is the value that has as many scores above it as it has below it, the 'middle'.

Methodology - The study or description of methods (e.g. in the social sciences).

Mode - This is the most frequently occurring value in a set of scores.

Multi-modal - Having many *modes.*

Negative correlation - Where one *variable* increases as the other decreases.

Nominal scale of measurement - This is when we use numbers to name objects and events in the world, e.g. a car registration number.

Normal distribution - A 'model' distribution of probabilities where many independent factors are acting at random.

Null hypothesis - This is the *hypothesis* that states that the most likely outcome of an investigation is that the results will be due to chance.

One-tailed alternate hypothesis - A *hypothesis* in which not only is a difference predicted but a specific difference (the direction of the difference) is predicted.

Order effect - This is an effect caused by the order in which the conditions in an experiment occur.

Ordinal scale of measurement - This is when we not only use numbers to identify objects or events we also put them in an order, e.g. competition places.

Phenomenology - The philosophical belief that our knowledge is based on our experience, on attending to phenomena as they are directly and subjectively experienced.

Population - The total number of people, objects, events or measurements sharing one or more features.

Positive correlation - Where one *variable* increases as the other variable increases.

Positivism - A philosophical idea that there is a fixed observable world which we all experience in a similar way. Knowledge is limited to observed facts and that which can be deduced from those facts.

Practice effect - This the sharp increase in performance due to the subjects needing a little time to get used to the procedure the experimenter is asking them to perform.

Predictive validity - We assess validity by trying to relate our measure to some future event, to predict its occurrence.

Primacy and recency effect - An effect due to the fact that people remember the first and last things in a list better than the middle things.

Psychometric tests - tests of psychological qualities such as personality variables, e.g. intelligence.

Qualitative - A non-numerical method which appreciates the characteristics or features of a person or event rather than a measurement of the size of those characteristics.

Quantitative - A numerical measurement of characteristics of people or events.

Random error - Errors that show their effect by chance.

Random sample - This is a *sample* selected by chance.

Random variables - Unpredictable variables affecting an experiment by chance.

Range - The difference between the highest and the lowest score.

Ratio scale of measurement - An interval scale of measurement, where not only are the intervals equal but there is a meaningful or absolute zero, e.g. length, temperature on the Kelvin scale.

Raw data - Data that is in its 'just collected' form and therefore unrefined and in need of organisation.

Reductionism - *Analysis* where an explanation is reduced to its simplest constituents.

Reliability - Also called *consistency*. It refers to the likelihood of getting the same results repeatedly if the measure is conducted in the same circumstances.

Repeated measures design - Experimental design where the same subjects are tested under both or all conditions.

Representative sample - This is a sample that contains within it all of the essential characteristics of the *population* from which it is drawn in the correct proportions.

Sample - Any part of a *population* specified by the person taking the sample.

Skew - The lack of symmetry in a *distribution* of scores.

Skewed distribution - This is where the bulk of the scores lies either to the right (positive skew) or to the left (negative skew) of the centre of the distribution.

Standard deviation - This is the square root of the *variance*.

Stratified sample - This sample is taken using the knowledge of the researcher of the characteristics of the *population*, e.g. age, sex, etc.

Symmetrical distribution - A distribution mirrored about its mid point.

Synthesis - Putting things together in familiar or novel ways to see what patterns are made and to understand how they might fit and work together.

Systematic sample - The sample is chosen according to a fixed method. (Though often still making the sample random within this system.)

Test-retest reliability -Taking of repeated measurements and *correlating* them.

Two-tailed alternate hypothesis - This type of hypothesis states that there will be an effect produced by the investigation and no more.

Validity - When a measure measures what it claims or intends to measure.

Variable - Anything that can vary, change and be measured.

Variance - The *mean* of the squared deviations from the mean.

Index